NO PLACE TO FALL

Also by Victor Saunders

Elusive Summits

NO PLACE TO FALL

SUPERALPINISM IN
THE HIGH HIMALAYA

Victor Saunders

Hodder & Stoughton
LONDON SYDNEY AUCKLAND

For Hugo and Ben

First published in 1994 by Hodder and Stoughton,
a division of Hodder Headline PLC.

British Library Cataloguing in Publication Data

Saunders, Victor
No Place to Fall: Superalpinism in the High Himalaya
I. Title
796.5

ISBN 0-340-57226-4

Typeset by Hewer Text Composition Services, Edinburgh
Printed and bound in Great Britain by
Mackays of Chatham plc

Hodder and Stoughton Ltd,
A division of Hodder Headline PLC
338 Euston Road
London NW1 3BH

Contents

Author's Acknowledgments

I should like to thank all those who helped set up these expeditions, travelled with me to the mountains and shared the exploration and the climbing, especially Steve Sustad who endured my company on all three trips. I am grateful to Chris Bonington, Ulric Jessop and Dick Renshawe for the loan of photographs indicated by their initials. All others are from my own collection.

I should also like to thank Harish Kapadia and his team from the Himalayan Club of Bombay for easing our passage in India and for their good company, and Mr S. P. Godrej for sponsoring our Panch Chuli expedition.

My thanks are due to my editor Maggie Body for frayed patience and, most of all, to my family for everything.

VS

PART ONE

MAKALU

1989

The Makalu Himal is situated in the Khumbakarna Himal, Nepal, about twelve miles east of Everest. Makalu (8481m) itself is the fifth highest peak after Everest (8848m), K2 (8611m), Kangchenjunga (8598m) and Lhotse (8511m). The main summit is sometimes referred to as Makalu I. Subsidiary peaks of the massif include the South-East Peak 8010 metres, Chomo Lonzo 7815 metres, Kangchungtse (Makalu II) 7640 metres, and Chago 6885 metres. According to Louis Baume the most probable origin for the name is Maha-kala, meaning in Tibetan "The Great Black One".

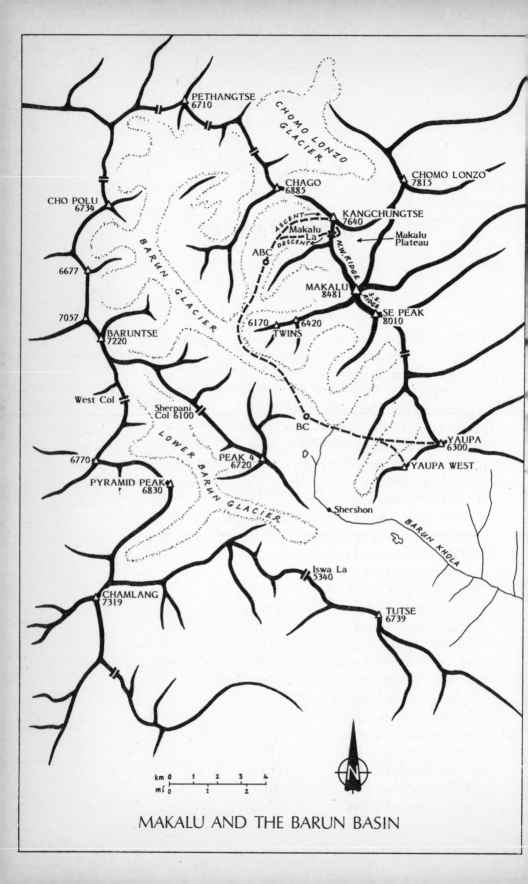

MAKALU AND THE BARUN BASIN

Chapter One

In the Beginning

It might have started in the pub. Most expeditions do. Maybe a chance mention of the mountain led to a beery response. Perhaps this led in turn to increasing enthusiasm, or a position difficult to back down from. One never remembers the details. Suddenly there is an expedition. Expeditions are like the full frontal storms of recent years, no one really knows how or where they start. On a South Pacific island a butterfly flaps its wings in a particular way. And a month later the entire south coast of England is devastated. If the insect had slept two minutes longer, we would have had perfectly clear cold winters, and the best ice climbing this century. There is a theory going the rounds of the popular science magazines that describes this sort of thing. It is all about instability, apparently. The theory calls itself Chaos Theory, and its proponents are known as chaologists. I find this highly descriptive of our expedition . . . Instability . . . Chaos.

And then again it might have started with a phone call.

"Blackspur? Never heard of them."

"Sell printers," said Andy Fanshawe, Fanny to his friends. "Big ones, they buy them second hand, do 'em up and sell them for mega millions. They're based here, in Manchester."

"And you think they might sponsor us?"

"Absolutely. We are going to meet the Marketing Director in the morning. You *are* coming up, aren't you? See you in Stockport." Clunk. Brrrrr. I was still looking at the handset. Speaking with Fanny was sometimes like being run over by a friendly locomotive.

The expedition was originally Mike Woolridge's idea. The team would not be one team, but four or five pairs of climbers. Base Camp was to be a shared facility. Snell's Field under Makalu. Should be cheap and cheerful, and the climbers would book enough routes on Makalu to keep everyone occupied without getting in each other's way. The team consisted of (in no discernible order, of course): Expedition Doctor – Gill Irvine, Hamish Irvine, Ulric Jessop, Andy Fanshawe, Rob Collister, Lindsay Griffin, Mike Woolridge, Calvin Torrans, Stephen Sustad, and myself.

Early in 1989 Mike and Lindsay were climbing in the Karakoram; they spent more time together that winter than they did with their respective spouses, so Fanny and I were left co-ordinating the fund-raising for the expedition.

Though we had booked no less than five different lines on the Makalu massif, the prime objective was the obvious one, the traverse of Makalu, and Stephen Sustad would be our Secret Weapon; he had already climbed to within metres of the summit by the night-marish South-East Ridge with Doug Scott and Jean Afanassieff. Their version of the South-East Ridge involved dropping into the world's highest hanging valley, and on retreat, trying to climb out of it again.

"It's like having to climb an 8000-metre peak just to get down," Steve had said with evident distaste. I had had the greatest difficulty persuading Steve to join the team but he agreed at least to look at the possibility of a traverse in the opposite direction, from north to south. Providing it was just the two of us climbing together. Providing the weather held out. And providing we felt sufficiently acclimatised. A tall order.

Part of the sponsorship package involved taking the media with us. There was a Video Team, Kees t'Hooft and Annette Carmichael.

Kees was one of my oldest friends, a Dutchman who'd settled in Clapham. I don't need to give a physical description: just think of Tintin, that's him, only no Snowy. Kees had a good track record for small-scale climbing documentaries, and was at the time at work editing adventure films in Soho. Annette worked for BBC Radio. They planned to shoot video footage of the climbing, with Annette doing the sound as well as Radio pieces. Kees took a copy of his latest video to Blackspur, who were impressed, and said they'd like to have one too. In addition to the video unit we had also acquired a film crew, Peter and Harriet Getzels, a combination guaranteed to increase the potential for entropy.

Fanny had been contacted by Peter Getzels who wanted to make an anthropological film about Sherpas and was looking for a convenient vehicle for this, and our expedition seemed to fit the bill.

We explained about Kees and Annette.

"There will be no conflict," Peter had said. "They will be living with you; we will be living with the Sherpas."

"Also," I added, "you understand that we are climbing alpine-style, we won't be using Sherpas as such. Only porters to base. Above Base Camp we'll be on our own. You won't be able to show Sherpas climbing with us."

"That's no problem."

Peter seemed very pleasant, humorous, and well informed on South American subjects. He was keen on the magico-realism of Marquez and Borges. Their South American documentary had won a prize. Good, I thought. We might have intelligent conversation on this expedition after all. Peter had lined up a production company called Passion Pictures who had a guaranteed fifty-minute slot on Channel Four. Our sponsor was ecstatic and everything was hunky-dory. Or so I thought.

Chapter Two

Monkey Business

In Kathmandu we picked up our Base Camp staff, two cooks, two assistant cooks, a sirdar, Nati, and our Liaison Officer, Mr Khanal of Interpol. All a normal part of the Nepalese conditions of permission. In addition to this the Getzels brought their daughter, Rachel, who in turn brought much joy to our Base Camp, and two nursery assistants, Annie the Nanny, and Tsering the Sherpani. So now there were the ten climbers, the seven media persons, the five Nepalese staff and the Liaison Officer. Already we were feeling the gale from the butterfly wings. We needed food and supplies for two months at base, and then there was the fortnight walk-in each way, three months' total food. That made about 120 porter loads, but the porters themselves needed food, and the porters carrying the porters' food needed food too, and so on *ad infinitum*. Actually not *ad infinitum*, otherwise Zeno would have been right. But our final porter-load tally was almost as large . . . 180, though we never had more than 140 porters. Round one to Chaology.

Hamish, Sue and I had flown out a week early to deal with the bureaucracy. Hamish was from Edinburgh. His maths degree had prepared him well for his current job, breeding trout near Aviemore. Hamish had been with Ulric Jessop and Fanny on the traverse of Chogolisa, and like them he was over six foot, full of muscle and horribly fit. Sue Hill made me feel tall, which is some accomplishment. Sue had written to Fanny during the winter. As a student of nutrition, she wanted to see how much food we ate and how much weight we lost during the trip. The result would be her final thesis. We didn't realise when we agreed to her joining our trip that we'd be filling in food diaries and weighing our intake every day.

For although she was small, she was fierce and strict, and it was not in our interests to be caught faking the data.

I said we went out early to battle with the bureaucrats, but we didn't realise that we were in fact to be battling with the elemental forces of nature. The universal slow-down, after the big bang, was starting in Kathmandu. Entropy was leaking out from the government buildings and slowly spreading across the town. Yes, entropy, the tendency to chaos, state of minimum potential energy. Events happened, if at all, in spasms; with long pauses in between; and had a tendency to unfold very, very slowly.

One by one the other team members arrived in town. We needed help to take on the enemy. Rob Collister, the most patient of the team, delegated himself to the freight clearance. Rob was a leading mountain guide. Patient and persistent, Rob was ideally suited to the task.

I knew that his father, a civil servant, had written a book about the British in Bhutan, and assumed that the Collister children had had a Himalayan childhood, but in fact they grew up in Kenya and Rhodesia. Rob had taken a long time to settle in the Principality of Wales. He stood a little taller than me, and was endowed with a large intelligent head, which became increasingly bearded. I supposed that in the colonial days Rob might have been one of those academic District Commissioners who spoke a dozen local languages and made elegant jokes in Latin and Greek.

Rob had one remaining ambition, to ascend an 8000m peak before growing too old. This was interesting, because his reputation was that of the consummate master of exploratory expeditions to lesser peaks. Rob was a latter-day Shipton; in an interview with the *Observer* newspaper, for the "Mountaineer's Mountaineer", Steve Venables had named Rob as his choice for that title. It had been a good choice, I thought.

To get expedition freight out of Customs was bureaucratic trench warfare. If the Indian subcontinent had learned their bureaucracy from the British, they applied it like Russian aparatchiks. Rob had to obtain letters and forms in nineteen-plicate, return them to the Ministry of Tourism, then to the Ministry of Culture, then back to Customs where the forms originated, and then round the circuit again. The Ministry of Culture was an apparently unfinished construction. Offices lined the corridors like monastic cells, cells which contained rickety school desks and piles and piles of paper.

"Oh no!" moaned Rob. "They've sent us back to desk number one again."

"How many are there?"

"Well, I got as far as desk four yesterday."

It was hot and airless. The functionaries dripped sweat as they laboriously read and reread every scrap of paper we placed before them. Lunch time went by. We would be pushed to make it to Customs the same day.

"You can enjoy the climbing . . ." – Rob continued an earlier conversation – "often in retrospect only, but if you don't reach the summit it lessens the pleasure. This must be true for all of us."

"Well, I think," I said, reaching deep into my memories, trying to reconstruct those moments I treasured, "I got more pleasure failing to climb Rimo I than topping out on Jitchu Drake."

Rob looked unconvinced. I went on.

"Mick Fowler once said that the best climbs are those where you either 'just' fail or 'just' succeed. It is the struggle that counts. I agree with him; I don't really have to stand on the top. When I climbed the Eiger, I realised my only climbing ambition. I had wanted to climb that face since I was thirteen years old, probably took up climbing in order to do it. It took me sixteen years. But the moment of elation was immediately followed by a tremendous sense of loss, loss of ambition, loss of direction, loss of . . ."

"Yes, I've heard other people say that, but I've never felt that myself."

Sometimes I feel that I am trying to run in thigh-deep treacle. I gave up the attempt, and we fell silent.

At three o'clock we were summoned to see the Acting Assistant Deputy Commissioner, who had a disconcertingly wide squint. Eyeing us both, one with each eye, he said that just as soon as we could produce a letter from Customs, we could receive our import licence.

"But we've already got the forms filled out and signed from the Customs Office. I thought we had finished." Rob looked like a man who had just watched his horse come in last.

"Just a two-line letter, requesting us to issue a licence." The Acting Assistant Deputy Commissioner dismissed us with a wave.

"OK," I said, "that's fine, we'll go to Customs and get another form."

"No!" said the Acting Assistant Deputy Commissioner, his eyes looking both sides of me. "You must get a letter!"

This was very interesting. We asked for a letter to Customs to explain to them what sort of letter they should write back to the Acting Assistant Deputy Commissioner. The bureaucratic machine ground to a halt. The Acting Assistant Deputy Commissioner looked distinctly unhappy, something very like exasperation clouded his face. An hour later we were taken to an office Rob had not seen before and presented with several pieces of paper which declared themselves to be Import Licences.

Stephen Sustad arrived in Kathmandu fresh, or I should say, worn out, from Doug Scott's trip to Rimo, where Steve and Nick Kekus had made the first ascent of Rimo II, and immediately took to bed with some indefinite lurgy. Kees flew in from London still hassling over the film contracts.

Our Liaison Officer arrived at the hotel. Although we were to call him Mister Khanal, he was an Inspector, in the employ of Interpol. Sustad looked up from his copy of *Viz*.

"It says here, 'Every day make a list of all the things you do and hand it in to the police station, then you will be eliminated easily from their inquiries in the event of a crime.' What about that, Mr Khanal, will that work for us?" Mr Khanal smiled sadly at Stephen's sense of humour.

"So you like to catch criminals?" I asked, trying to add dignity to the conversation.

"Oh no! I like to sit behind my desk. I do not like to catch criminals, I send other men to catch criminals. I am a bureaucrat. I have a desk job." Mr Khanal grinned happily. He was always smiling, and the world smiled with him. We were to find our Liaison Officer had a heart of pure solid gold.

Peter and Harriet hired their Sherpani. Tsering was in effect an assistant nanny; her job was to carry Rachel during the trek. She was also very pretty, as our sirdar Nati had obviously noticed. Nati was young and smart, with straight black hair, new jeans and dazzling sun-glasses, and he always lolled in a slightly more nonchalant way when Tsering appeared.

That summer Kathmandu was a wonderful place to be. Between the expedition jobs, buying, packing and extracting goods from Customs, we found time to enjoy the city. Stephen and I often ate at the Kushi Fuji, a real Japanese restaurant where it was difficult to break the two-pound-a-head barrier. The flavours of Japanese food were as thin and delicious as rarefied mountain air. I sat cross legged on the tatami enjoying a full belly while the monsoon rain drummed on the restaurant roof. Stephen picked over his remaining vegetarian Tempura.

"Yup," he said munching contentedly. "Kathmandu. You're right. It *is* one of the Great Flesh Pots of the world."

There was the Old Vienna run by a Swiss and an Austrian. Marco Polo provided Mediterranean fare, Pumpernickel's had Teutonic breads. There were countless "veggie" restaurants (best avoided), and an equal number of pizza places (avoid like the plague), Korean, Chinese and no less than five Japanese restaurants. There were Indian restaurants, Nepali restaurants, coffee places, safe ice-cream parlours, American breakfast places – in a sentence, everything except English food. Sustad, an expatriate Scandinavian American, claimed there were no English restaurants abroad, anywhere.

I was puzzled. Why had all these immigrants settled here? Some were easy to understand, such as those who remained in Nepal after their military careers, eking out a living on pension and trek organising. But what about the owners of the Old Vienna? They were more Austrian than the Austrians. And what about the legendary Liz Hawley? She was said to be encyclopaedic about Himalayan history. Originating from Chicago, and a former researcher for *Fortune* magazine, she had been in Nepal twenty years, first as a Reuters stringer, then, when the Nepali government removed her accreditation, working with Mountain Travel.

I had visited her with Kees. Her business card declared her to be a correspondent for a clutch of climbing magazines and journals. Liz was no mountaineer. She considered her relationship to mountaineering as being that of a chronicler. Nothing else. She was not, nor ever had been, interested in climbing for herself. Not even trekking. In fact she rarely went closer to the mountains she wrote about than Kathmandu.

"Yes," she said, smacking her dry lips like a fish gasping for air, "two Poles and one Mexican summited Makalu last year. Here is the list of summiteers. Sixty-three in total."

"But one of these Poles died on the way down," I pointed out.

"Died? Died? Let me see, list of Expeditions to Makalu – 1988 – Polish – Deaths: one – yes, here it is."

"Do you know the mortality rates for the big peaks?" I was a little bit intrigued; the mistress statistician went on.

"Two point five per cent for climbers above Base Camp, but I am still having data typed into the computer. When we're through we'll be able to produce the figures in greater detail."

Taking our leave we nearly stepped on a hairy terrier which had been skulking under a coffee table.

"Mallory! Come here!" Liz barked as we shut the door behind us.

It was early August, a time when you can buy almost anything in Kathmandu except Vaseline. Vaseline was necessary, said Lindsay, as a leech protective. You worked it with salt and rubbed the goo all over your gaiters; this was meant to keep the little creatures from climbing up your legs. Sustad said leeches were heat seekers. They stood on rocks vertically, the heads bent towards the source of warmth as it passed. When there were several on a rock, I supposed the leeches must resemble a tennis crowd. I had yet to discover whether leeches moved by a series of scissors movements, or by somersaulting. In any case they didn't crawl, because they used only their heads and tails for locomotion.

It was also mid-monsoon, and the afternoons tended to be wet, but in the mornings we usually ran into Roger Mear. Although his reputation was based on his walk to the South Pole, he was a real mountaineer's mountaineer with an early winter ascent of the Eiger and the first winter ascent of the Cassin Ridge to his credit. (He was to go on to make a fine alpine-style ascent of Nanga Parbat with Dave Walsh two years later.) The best thing about Roger, though, was that he was the same height as me: I could walk down the streets of Kathmandu with Roger and not feel dwarfed.

Roger and Paul Rose formed the English contingent of the Anglo-American Everest expedition, going round to the Chinese side. With them was Rebecca Stephens, a Sloane Ranger covering the expedition for *The Times*, who seemed extraordinarily out of place. Surrounded by unwashed climbers, without her twinset and pearls. During the expedition she climbed to 7600 metres, a brilliant feat for a complete beginner. Which all went to prove how deceptive appearances can be. (Rebecca became the first British woman to climb Everest in 1993.)

We were almost ready to leave town, and had a spare day to explore. Kees and I made our only touristic journey in the city. Till then there had only been two kinds of journey from the hotel room, business and food. Tourism was a whole new class of journey. We hired a pair of old black boneshakers with seemingly solid iron wheels. Armed with a tourist map of Kathmandu we became instantly and irretrievably lost. There were bazaars everywhere, all the shop-filled alleys looked exactly the same. We found ourselves on the outskirts of town, under a small hill on top of which stood a glistening white and gold gompa. Cycling in Kathmandu is just as arbitrary as casting yarrow stalks; we had not meant to come here, but perhaps we had been guided. This was the Monkey Temple. Two hundred and fifty stone steps, steep and worn, climbed straight up to the temple gates. Small shrines bordered the stairway holding offerings of petals and ochre powder. The monkeys, no larger than domestic cats, chattered and fidgeted while we laboured on the steps. Two hundred and fifty steep steps is a long way, equivalent to twenty tower-block floors. We were puffing like pensioners on arrival, but the climb had its reward. We found ourselves in a complex of shrines, gold-plated stupas and whitewashed chortens. Butter lamps, and copper prayer cylinders burnished with use, were arranged around the central stupa in sentry boxes. Monkeys and Italian tourists (a coach must have just arrived) overran the place. Pilgrims laid food in the laps of the Buddhas, which the monkeys promptly removed. The monkeys here lead a secure and fecund life. Several of them had hamster-sized babies clinging to their breasts.

There was a droning noise from behind a chorten which turned out to be a monk performing a puja before a shrine, scattering rice and spices into small dishes. Hum-drone-Om-Mani-Padme-Hum-drone. He rang a brass handbell and added butter to the lamps. Black and shiny, the prayer beads rippled through his left hand. Incense and sandalwood perfumed the slight breeze. Behind the monk, the sun, as sharp as a Chirico, split the whitewashed chortens into abstract shapes, broken only by a flurried speckle of rock doves disturbed by the monkeys. Beneath the temple on the steep hillside, troops of tumbling monkeys played in a grove of acacia. And down below the trees was Kathmandu, a town about the size of Hyde Park, spread out in the afternoon light under a blanket, a haze of hearth smoke.

Somewhere in that haze, Stephen was offered a shoeshine. He always wore trainers, and had never been accosted by a shoeshine before. This was a completely new experience.

"How much?" he asked.

"Ten rupees." It was about twenty pence.

"OK," said Stephen. "You shine your own shoes, I'll watch." Stephen paid the money and sat down. The man carefully unpacked an old wooden box. He put out a bottle of spirit the colour of blood, then unwrapped a scrubbing brush which had lost most of its hairs. Stephen bummed a spare beedie from the shoeshine and watched

him buff his own shoes. "He did a real good job. He found it
amusing. I found it amusing."

The next day the team embarked on the expedition bus. We
were heading for one of those horrible Himalayan twenty-four-hour
journeys that never find their way into literature.

Chapter Three

To the Barun Valley

There was a truck for the loads, and a dilapidated bus with flea-infested seat cushions for the team. It took all day to load the truck. After five hours of bumping, grinding and swinging through hairpin bends out of Kathmandu, the infernal machine stopped at a smoke-blackened chai house where a green parrot squawked in Nepali until the cook gave it a red chilli to eat. The parrot held the pepper in one claw, crunching the fruit and chattering. I looked closely at the bird to see if it showed any signs of the searing pain that eating the chilli would have produced in me. No. No weeping eyes, no gasping for water. Strange.

I clutched the tiny enamel cup of sweet tea and watched two bantams screech and tear at each other with their karate heel-hooks, till one of them noticed a spillage of rice on the ground and began pecking. The other cock followed suit and in an instant the enemies were table mates. They were almost flattened as a bus-load of Catalan climbers arrived at the chai house, also bound for Makalu, and racing us to Hille. The first expedition always got the pick of the porters.

We tried to sleep overnight in the bus; it was impossible. We might as well have been inside a tumble dryer. Even at night the air was hot and the flea bites had begun to itch. By morning we had left the plains of Nepal, the Terai, and had begun the long haul up into the foothills. We were heading for the Arun valley in east Nepal. Our route was to follow the lower reaches of this ancient stream.

From the Kangshung Glacier, under the East Face of Everest, the Kama Chu flows clockwise round the Makalu massif, cutting a deep gorge through the mountains to become, once across the border, the Arun river. As the mountains grew, so the river cut deeper, preserving a pattern of flow that predated the headlong and reckless crash of India into Asia, one of the few rivers to traverse the Himalaya.

As the sun rose the temperature inside the vehicle soared. It was more comfortable to ride with the luggage on top of the bus. Ulric discovered this possibility when a flapping tarpaulin needed fixing and the driver, laughing maniacally, could not be persuaded to stop.

The road ended in a muddy street lined with dark, sinister shop fronts and fly-filled chai houses. Hille. When the awful bus rattled in, the clouds parted briefly, long enough for Mike to see Makalu 100 miles away. Five miles high and ten miles wide. Had I seen it, I would have turned for home there and then.

The Catalan team had arrived at Hille before us. Their bus driver must have been even more lunatic than ours. Mike, Fanny, and Mr Khanal made a deal with their opposite numbers to fix the porter rates at 50 rupees per day, with a day's advance per porter. Two hours later the Catalan had settled at a daily rate of 60 rupees, with an advance payment of 150. Of course, we had to follow suit, and I saw Mike calculating on a sheet of paper. "That's going to cost us another £200," he said.

Our official head porter was a twenty-year-old called Pasang, who had the air of a well-mannered but slightly ineffectual junior officer. The man who made the whole thing work was Lapka Dorji, whom we had originally hired as a mail runner; he organised the men like an NCO. But they needed each other: Lapka couldn't write in English, and Pasang was reasonably fluent.

Meanwhile Kees was being educated by Ravindra Singh, a teacher of science who had been visiting Chainpur. Kees, a keen student of the Vedas, wondered if the visit could have been a possible pilgrimage. I looked on with interest.

Kees   Where do you teach?
RS   Solu Kumbhu, I teach in Solu.
Kees   Why were you in Chainpur?
RS   Yes, in Chainpur, then in Changwan.
Kees   But why?
RS   Why?
Kees   Yes, why in Chainpur?
RS   Then I go to Changwan and reach there at two o'clock.

Kees   But what reason did you have for visiting Chainpur?
RS   Reason? Ah, reason?
Kees   Reason – In – Chainpur? (He could not have put it more clearly, or slowly either.)
RS   Buddhism.
Kees   Buddhism? (Intriguing!)
RS   Because reason in Chainpur is Buddhism. Reason in Hille is Hindu. Reason in Changwan is Hindu. My reason is Hindu. Your reason is?

If it was difficult to sleep on the bus, it was almost worse in Hille. The so-called hotel was basic, and infested, but that was not the problem. We were used to that. What really surprised me was the rampaging pack of mongrels who began to howl and terrorise the street after dark. Sustad referred to them affectionately as "disco dogs" but I noticed that he did not risk going out for a pee.

Then just as I fell asleep, there was the most god-awful noise. I awoke dreaming that a rusty cow was refusing to be slaughtered, but it was only the local lama and his assistants blowing on horns and dispelling evil spirits at each door. "The last time we were here the lamas banged their drums all night," said Sustad. I wondered if in some way he embodied the evil spirit they were trying to ward off.

We were already outflanked on the daily porter rates, but the men of Hille had an even better scam. Not only did they play off the expeditions in town against each other, but there was the giant-Korean-expedition-arriving-next-day trick. The Koreans would be needing no less than 600 porters, and if we did not settle with the Hille contractors at a favourable price, we'd get no porters at all. "It's just like the stock market," said Calvin. "We'll have to start a counter-rumour. How about the-Korean-expedition-permit-has-just-been-cancelled?" Soon after this particular rumour began to circulate, our first porters announced themselves.

My job for the morning was to note the name and village of each of our prospective porters. I was struck by the variety of ethnic groups. Some described themselves as "tribes"; these groups were mostly Hindu, and included the Rai, Chetri, Bishukarma and Bavus. The Buddhist groups tended to describe themselves as a "people"; they included Sherpa, Bhotia and Tamang. The Newari men described themselves to me as being either Buddhist or Hindu or both or neither. Each man I asked gave a different reply. I couldn't quite make it out, perhaps they thought it was fun to tease us. Ulric had his own theory, thereby revealing the bizarre world inside his head.

"The uncertainty principle states that if you know they are Newari, you can't know what religion they are, and the converse must be that if you *do* know what religion they are, you can't be certain they are Newari." He paused a moment, leant his head to one side and said, "Have you asked all the others if they know they are *not* Newari?"

Meanwhile Stephen pointed to Annie the Nanny and Tsering walking through the village holding hands.

"It looks like Nati is out of luck," said Stephen, observing the first rule of gossip: always leap to conclusions.

From Hille we walked for three days along the river banks, a walk which Hugh Swift's *Trekker's Guide* describes as unpleasantly hot and humid, so hot, in fact, that in order to sleep, we were forced to take midnight swims and lie naked on the river banks under damp towels. In this part of the Arun valley, the Rai villages resembled the Malayan kampongs of my childhood, and the women wore spectacular nose and ear jewellery.

There were chai stops every half-hour at first. Here the Rais were dark-skinned Hindus. They lived in simple dwellings, framed with two-storey-high poles. Americans call this system of building balloon framing. The roof was a thatch made from rice stalks. An open-weave bamboo matting formed the walls. The ground floor was defined, like a kampong, only by the stilts, and provided rudimentary shelter from sun and rain for the animals. The living area was raised an arm's reach above the head and supported on round beams.

This is the archetype, and exists at the 500-metre altitude. Above 1000 metres, on the ridges above the river, the bamboo matting at first-floor level is covered with mud to give it a little weather resistance. At 2000 metres the open "ground floor" area acquires weather-resistant wattle and daub. Finally at the highest villages the space between the posts is filled with dry-stone walling.

The base of the Arun is too hot for leeches, but above 2000 metres, is prime leech country. As the path climbed higher the chai stops became rarer, and Mani wall and prayer flags indicated the Buddhism of the population. At the village of Bhotibas we found Ongyal our cook being scolded by his mother. When he saw us he looked studiously away from her, and talked to us pretending his mother was just some woman passing by. But they were in fact standing at the entrance to the family house and to Ongyal's obvious embarrassment his mother brought out chang. All round his house bright green rice terraces were cascading down the hillsides; transient vapour clouds drifted through the narrow valleys. We took time to watch the view, stunned. So beautiful. What a place to live. No television, no videos. No Walkman, for me at least. I wanted to hear the sounds of the forest. At night I lay awake and listened to the rain on the tent, the distant torrent and the wind in the trees.

The fourth day stage, to Chichila, was to take the team six hours, and the load carriers ten hours. The path ran through jungle for a few miles, then out into slash-and-burn territory again. The burnt zone was fended off with bamboo matting and turned over to grazing. Later the tree stumps would be grubbed up and the hillside terraced for agriculture. Although the forest, and all it contained, was thereby reduced, there did not seem to be much obvious evidence of soil erosion. There were few scars on the Arun valley hillsides, and the few landslides I did see looked to have occurred in uncut jungle.

The monsoon was enjoying a vigorous day when the team reached Chichila. It was like standing under a tap. But the path through the forest had been on red clay, and this thixotropic material turned to soap when wet. Several load bearers were caught out in the rain and the dark. Hamish and Ulric organised a rescue party.

The porters were two kilometres back, in the darkest part of the jungle. Ulric decided this was the moment to try out the porters' head-strap method of carrying loads; he would have gone out barefoot had we not stopped him. He strode out into the night. Hamish was still trying to call him back when there was a loud, and distressingly long, crashing sound accompanied by a wonderful variety of colourful oaths; Ulric was dragged head first by his load through the steep and leech-infested undergrowth. Even when we got Ulric out of the black jungle, muddy, bruised and hung about with leeches, he refused to accept that for us Europeans, using a rucksack might be simpler.

The fifth stage, from Num to Shedowa, was famous. It was both the shortest day and the hardest. It involved a horizontal distance of a mile. You could easily see the other village, but the two were separated by a gorge a mile deep. On the long climb up to Shedowa, Kees and Ulric tried to gauge their progress by reference to Num. It never seemed to work, the next hour always took two, the next thirty minutes took an hour. At length Kees announced:

"You never are as high as you think you are."

"Then it follows," said Ulric, "that if you are as high as you think, you must have underestimated the distance."

Walking up to Shedowa we were in Sherpa country. Here at last was virgin rain forest. Here too we met Annie who was in tears. The path up to Shedowa was steep and long, and Tsering was slowing down, so Annie offered to carry Rachel for Tsering, but was told by Harriet that would be patronising, and that Annie was being too macho. Moreover, Harriet had added, Annie was corrupting the Sherpa culture with lesbianism.

Beyond Shedowa was Navagon, a sub-village of Tashigon. This was where our head porter lived. Pasang's house had been built by Chetri builders from Khanbari. Pasang explained: "Sherpa people not so good with big houses, not thinking good . . ." He tapped his head. Pasang's family paid 5000 rupees (about £100, though English money doesn't really translate in a self-sufficient society) for the structure, but provided the labour themselves. So there was a caste system for building in the Arun alley. I am told that in Khumbu the Sherpas do their own building.

Over the fireplace a wooden trellis for smoking meat shone black with accumulated tar in the lasers of sunlight which speared the smoke. A fifteen-year-old girl, who looked nine, helped Pasang's sister prepare chang. The girl was the daughter of a poor neighbour, and had been indentured for five years in exchange for a payment of 500 rupees.

After the chang, which was warm and sour, Pasang went to the gompa and there Pasang's father and half a dozen other lamas were conducting a white puja. Pasang's father was the head lama. The Sherpa lamas appeared not to have shaved at all. Their hair was tied into a thick matted pony-tail, up to a metre long. The white puja was, Pasang said, the third and final puja after a death. The deceased had been an eighty-year-old woman. The assembled inhabitants of Navagon had been performing the puja for the last twenty-four hours with only chang and a clear white spirit, raksi, for sustenance. The raksi was delicious, but I couldn't quite place the familiar taste, so I took another bowl. And after several more bowls I was able to identify the resemblance; it was like very strong sake, or perhaps vodka. No, I couldn't be sure; another bowl please.

The row of lamas rang brass hand bells and droned prayers from rolled scriptures, throwing spices occasionally at the butter lamps. The chang and raksi had begun to take their toll. One of the lamas was asleep and had fallen sideways against Pasang's father. Back in her own house, Pasang's mother was nursing a very sore head. Pasang and I staggered back up to Tashigon.

Fortunately it was not far to Tashigon, the last permanent habitation on our trek. But the path lay through leech jungle which put our various remedies to the test. Lindsay had smeared salted Vaseline on his legs, Nati marinaded his in chilli sauce while Lapka painted his thick bare legs with bright orange Sherpa tobacco, which comes in damp sachets, and is probably the world's most foul-smelling substance. Something like canned skunk. Nothing worked; we all streamed with blood.

Gill Irvine, our extremely sanguine expedition doctor, declared the bites to be harmless, provided we avoided infection. Where do they train them? I mean how is it that all expedition doctors I have ever known seem to have had a compassion-ectomy?

Tashigon was the last village in the fortnight trek. We had covered almost half the 150 kilometres in distance and in time. Here we were due to change the valley porters for mountain porters, in other words, to swap our mixed retinue of Hindus and lowland Buddhists for highland Sherpas. This was the tradition, the alternative was to suffer a porter strike. Or so we were told. We had the benefit of both.

We blamed the Catalan effect on market forces again. For a while things looked ugly, sticks were waved, but the angry porters were directing their gestures at Lapka and Nati, not us. When the ululation at last died down our kitchen staff, who were mostly Sherpas, held a song and dance, and produced six enormous kettles of chang. Sustad got horribly drunk and forced us all to dance, but he paid for it with a sore head that made him look like Pasang's mother. In the morning Mike took one look at him and said:

"You should see your eyes, mate, they look like a mad dog's bollocks."

"It's the milk in the tea," said Steve. "It's given me a headache too."

Steve and Fanny spent the next day noting the new porters who were all Sherpas bar three Rais, one of whom, Ravindra Rai, spoke English with a beautiful idiolect:

"Excuse me, sir, ah, would it be possible for me to carry a load for you?"

Pasang and Lapka Dorji said they didn't like Ravindra because "he gets angry and starts fighting". I couldn't help wondering if being a Rai in a Sherpa village might not lead one to anger and fighting.

Very early the next morning the full complement of Sherpa load bearers, including several Sherpanis who smelled nicely of woodsmoke and walked barefoot in spite of the leeches, began to file out of the campsite. Annie was wandering around looking at the ground near her tent, in the sort of distraught state only those working with small children could understand. ". . . And now one of my socks has completely disappeared." Hamish called out from inside his tent, "Have you checked you haven't got two on one foot?" "Oh, hmm," said Annie looking sheepish and trying to hide one foot behind the other.

Above Tashigon the route gained height. The thirty-metre chestnuts, beech and oak began to thin out. Thick clumps of bamboo took over the open spaces beneath the canopy. Over a ridge, onto a slightly more westerly aspect of slope, the species changed abruptly. Now we toiled among the twisted rhododendron. Gnarly red trunks reached for space and passing rucksacks.

It began to rain again, and we tried to erect the umbrellas, but they kept catching in the branches. It poured. We found ourselves walking on two colours of Himalayan balsam flowers, and a strange pink strawberry, Dalton's strawberry, which turned out to be slightly less palatable than wet blotting paper.

A four-hour climb above Tashigon was Ongen, the camp for the evening, a fantastic place, an escarpment with steep cliffs and caves on all sides which the porters quickly occupied. Fanny, a geologist by education, became extremely excited. "It's classic horst uplift," he said. "With layered basalt, you can tell because . . ." I was unable to follow the rest, it was not in layman's language.

We were now in yak country. It occurred to us that yaks should do very well in the Cairngorms. It was just like this. Cold, wet, windy and boggy. The monsoon rain poured by the bucketful, and although, at 4000 metres, we were now above the leech forests, several of us had brought fellow travellers with us. Smoke issued from the hidden caves, betraying the hideouts of the load bearers. Ravindra Rai put down his load and said, "If it pleases you, sir, I am now going to my shelter. Ha ha. To my den."

The next day took the team over Shipton's Col (c. 4400m), from where there is supposed to be a fine view of Makalu. Even though nothing bar mist and bog was to be seen, all felt a sense that the watershed had been crossed. Then the path descended to the Barun valley where our base was to be. This was the home stretch. The pass was marked with prayer flags, and below the watershed was a misty lake with a cairn in the middle of it, stuck with bamboo poles, more prayer flags and offerings of leaves and flowers.

The bog gave way to willow scrub, then low rhododendron bushes, which turned into trees as the path descended once more into the leech forests. Above the tree-line I stopped in a momentary lapse in the weather. The sun glimmered on the wet bushes, a high keening sound hung in the air, a pair of soaring birds rode the currents above a line of red crags. A tiny soprano "chip chip chip" radiated from a willow. I shut my eyes to listen better, but heard instead the galumphing slap of trainers on damp earth, accompanied by a buzzing, drizzling noise. I opened my eyes. The buzzing was a Walkman turned up to the max. Fanny steamed past, grinning hugely, and said, "Nice view, eh? Way to go!" waved, and was gone, stomping down the road.

The Barun valley must be one of the most beautiful valleys I had ever seen. It was the landscape dreams are made of. Granite walls enclosed a pastoral ribbon, conifers decorated the edges, waterfalls cascaded in 100-metre leaps; grazing herds of yak, and the lone herder's hut with the traditional Sherpa bamboo matting roofs, were the only signs of habitation. Two days after crossing Shipton's Col we reached our base. Two days during which we followed this beautiful strip of fertile soil through the tree-line, into Alpine pastures, and finally past the last herder's outpost of Sherson, where Sustad was already supping yak yogurt, to a grassy knoll across the Barun river on the side of an ancient lateral moraine where our base was to be.

Annette had begun to feel the altitude. We were now at 4500 metres, and Puree, our kitchen boy, happily added her rucksack to his own load, and Mr Khanal thought perhaps that Annette should go down. But he was wrong. She just acclimatised slowly, and so had the celebrated Jerzy Kukuczka who climbed all fourteen 8000-metre peaks. But Annette was a conscientious worker, recording everything that passed, logging all her entries. She was good at her job. Often when the team was deep in conversation I noticed out of the corner of an eye Annette's microphone unobtrusively listening in too. The trek had also accustomed us to the Getzels' filming style. They like to use a wide-angle lens on their Aaton, and get right into the action. This meant having them pop up between you and whoever you were talking to. I am told that shows commitment.

Later Pasang, as trainee lama, performed the puja for the new camp. We all threw rice to the wind with great joyous shouts. As the unpacking proceeded, the waste was set aside for burning at the conclusion of the trip. It happens to be very bad karma to burn rubbish while a camp is in use. At the head of the camp there was now a tall prayer flag and a stone altar for burnt offerings. The team had been at base for an hour when the monsoon clouds parted briefly to show first a fragment, then the whole of the South Face of Makalu. It wasn't *over* there, it was *up* there. The face was so high and so large we had to crane our necks to look at it. Like an apparition floating in the clouds, the summit hovered two miles above our heads. I know what fear is. I felt it then.

Chapter Four

To the Makalu La and Dreams

Our mess tent was designed to house twenty people, and was an architectural masterpiece. Annie the Nanny said so, and she should know. In term time she was a staff photographer at the Architectural Association.

I designed the structure, a poplar "A" frame. The ridge was a length of 5 mm cord tied to a highish boulder behind, and a buried stone in front. Stephen, as team carpenter, detailed the joints of the frame, but it was Mr Khanal, who had a dextrous kukri, who fashioned the joints. Mike sewed orange and blue tarpaulins together to make the roof; so under the diffused light we looked either sick or ill depending on which side we sat.

Ulric and Hamish, the team mathematicians, completed the mess by tensioning out the sides with fiendishly complicated contraptions of twisted wood and contorted tin boxes. We constructed toilets, dug pits for rubbish and wet slops, and collected about two porter loads of rubbish from the site. Our site was bad, but the outwash plain below the camp was worse, strewn with tin cans and foil wrappers that previous expeditions had apparently expected to disappear of their own accord. Last of all we set up a long table of food boxes down the middle.

While the cooks constructed a dry-stone wall kitchen, complete with shelving and sitting stones, we unpacked. Most of the loads had survived the monsoon. But Kees found that both his barrels had somehow become waterlogged. His clothes and electronic equipment were wet through. Surprisingly the electronics were unaffected, but the clothes had become mouldy. For the rest of the expedition you could always tell when Kees was approaching because he was preceded by a slight odour of mushroom. Even his inexhaustible supply of fine Dutch cigars failed to perfume over completely the fungoid smell of his duvet.

There were rice, pasta, potatoes, jams, chocolate powder and sweets. There were spices, sauces, instant cheese mixes and dehydrated meals. As we worked, sorting out the stores, we listened to the radio. By lunch England were 114 for 6, chasing 420. Atherton had fallen between the peanut butter and the marmalade, while Fairbrother failed at the tinned curry and old Goochie failed to outlast the Marmite. "We'll be forced to follow on," we muttered blackly. Sustad looked at us in pity and shook his American head.

At the last packet of instant mash the radio announced, "We've avoided the follow-on by fourteen runs!" There were audible sighs of relief from Lindsay and me, while Stephen looked up long enough to display a pitying smirk.

That evening, the first at base, Steve and I recrossed the river for an acclimatising walk to spend the night at 5400 metres, with thunderous headaches for me, and mild interest from Sustad, who said he had never suffered from headaches in the mountains. "Except after milk?" I asked. I gave up with the headaches, and returned to base the next day. Our acclimatising was characterised by frequent returns to base. And each time we came home there was news of the others. It was rather like a protracted chess game in which we made our move, then had to find out what the others had done. Acclimatisation for extreme altitude is like a Victorian courtship. Woe betide the eager suitor who bounds straight in with the ring. You have to serve time laying metaphorical bunches of red roses on the lesser summits while awaiting the moment when the weather relents enough to give you permission to address your chosen bride in form.

This time Kees had pains in his chest; Gill said she might have to take him down to a lower altitude. When next we returned, Gill had diagnosed pleurisy and had gone down the valley with Kees. Meanwhile Andy returned alone from a foray, leaving Mike, Lindsay and Calvin somewhere on the Barun Glacier. He had suddenly decided to take Nati and the video camera up Peak 4, an elegant ice peak with steep rock buttresses, two hours from our camp.

After breakfast Andy and Nati packed their sacks for Peak 4. Steve and I prepared our equipment for Yaupa Central (6300m) which, as far as the records went, had not been climbed before. I had packed our food into plastic sandwich bags, one for each day, and collected all the evening meals into one stuff sack, the breakfast in another. All pretty logical, I thought. At length Sustad could hold himself back no longer: "Getting organised? Getting organised? To be organised is a sign of insanity!"

Sustad's methods require some explanation: to pack food for a five-day outing, grab five pounds of assorted food, throw into stuff sack, sit back and enjoy serendipity. You never know what will be pulled out at each meal. This, of course, is the sign of perfect sanity.

During lunch Mike, Lindsay and Calvin returned from their esoteric explorations. It was never possible to find out exactly where Lindsay had been.

"Oh, just somewhere over there, old boy."

"Please be more specific."

"Somewhere specifically over there. Will that do?"

Meanwhile, to add to the general chaos, our cook Mingma took ill. Andy emerged from Mingma's tent and announced his diagnosis to the crowd of Sherpas, filmers and climbers:

"Acute mountain sickness. He'll have to go down as soon as possible."

Steve was next. He put his head inside the tent, and when he finished he turned to the assembly and said loudly:

"Appendicitis! His pain is in the left side of his stomach. I wonder if he has developed peritonitis yet?"

Mike finished his lunch, strolled over to Mingma's tent, where the poor Sherpa was groaning, and called for silence. He ordered everyone out of Mingma's tent, produced paper and encil, and began to take notes. "Eyes? Bad taste in the mouth? Pain here? Here? Temperature? Pulse? Diarrhoea?" After quarter of an hour he finished. He stood up outside the tent and said:

"Probably got a touch of flu. Just aspirins for now. Gill will be back tomorrow."

Mingma was not persuaded by the aspirin. The next morning a Sherpa lama was in front of Mingma's tent, performing a puja, scattering rice to all corners of the compass. Inside, a very sorrowful Mingma crouched at the back of the tent, looking balefully at the lama. I patted the bottom of Mingma's sleeping bag and he burst into tears. It was then that Mr Khanal explained all.

Mingma had been having dreams. He was also Nati's brother, and was frightened about Nati climbing with Andy. The Sherpa lama added that this was a very bad campsite, and every year without fail, some Sherpa or climber would die here. "No one was hurt when I was here in 1984," said Sustad quietly, but the Sherpas ignored him. The point was that if Nati went up Peak 4 there would be some very bad karma. Possibly a fatality. Andy decided the best thing was to leave Nati in camp – though it was true Nati had been looking forward to climbing – to join Steve and me for the Yaupa climb.

I never discovered why Andy wanted to climb Peak 4 with Nati. Perhaps it was to do with our film unit. It had gradually transpired that the Getzels were intending to produce a film showing how Western climbers had misused Sherpas over the years. Their film synopsis painted a picture of big traditional siege-style expeditions; a picture of Sherpas doing all the high-altitude climbing and the Sahibs getting the rewards. They wanted to make an exploitation movie. Unfortunately we were not taking any high-altitude porters, so how did they intend to shoot the footage of Sherpas climbing? "No problem," their producer at Passion Pictures had said: "We'll equip your sirdar with climbing gear and he can climb with Peter."

As we waddled out of base after an enormous lunch, we wondered if Mingma's dreams meant anything. Was it simple superstition? Or were our friends on the mountain really in trouble? Hamish returned from the Chago Glacier, leaving Ulric to climb Chago (6860m) alone. Gill arrived from the lower valley with the news that Kees would follow in a couple of days. Peter and Rob were still somewhere "up there" in the high glaciers around Baruntse on a Journey of Discovery. Who was in danger?

Andy and Steve were much fitter than me, so I went first as we crossed the glacier. The mist closed up all horizons, and it was difficult to tell where the crevasses might be. I have a morbid fear of crevasses, so I was moving with some care. Sustad said that avalanches were his *bête noire*, slots were no problem at all, provided you were on a rope. "Victor, you need to fall into a slot once or twice, roped, and you'd get over your fear." I was not so sure, and apologised for moving so slowly. Steve replied, 'It's OK, Andy and I are hopping along on one leg."

We slept on the glacier under Yaupa that night. All three of us crammed into a two-man Gemini. We had a version of the tiny tent with an experimental snow entrance at the back. This was a circular affair, just large enough to crawl through, about the same diameter as a sleeping bag. We found a use for this by making Andy sleep with legs in the snow entrance and his head inside the tent, where we spoon-fed him soup, drinking chocolate and cheese lumps.

The climb of Yaupa Central was a one-day effort, mostly in the mist. There was no view from the summit. The gale we had climbed in blew up into a minor storm, while I developed all the signs of acute dysentery; an inconvenient combination made worse by the coarse jokes of my companions. We were overtaken by dusk as we fixed the last of our two abseils. The spinning snow whipped across the face, blowing the ropes out sideways, and forced us to duck into the hoods of our anoraks. I placed the abseil pegs with numbed frozen fingers, the head torch casting a dim and wobbly light on the crack, while I clenched at my even more wobbly bowels; I must admit to a perverse thrill. This was the first real sense of urgency on this trip. Strange to say, I quite enjoyed it when things felt serious. So did Sustad, but then you'd expect him to like unpleasant things. And then after the abseils, there were more unhappy attempts to relieve the bowels into the storm. And there, cackling and smirking at my misfortune, like the witches on the blasted heath, my companions. What a way to spend your summer holiday.

By the time we staggered back to base I hadn't eaten for two days. Mingma made tomato soup and cheese samosas. He had been fully cured by the passing lama. For this Mike and Nati had paid the man fifty rupees each. Actually the lama had been trying to sell bananas to the expedition when Mingma took ill, and medicine was only a sideline to his banana trading. Hamish had the poor taste to dub him the Banana Lama. More of Hamish's sense of humour later, though less may be preferable.

Of the seven team members away from base immediately after Mingma's dream, five were now safe. Steve, Andy and I were home. Kees was fully cured. Ulric had soloed Chago, and returned having lost nothing but his voice. He always lost his voice at altitude, and later that afternoon Rob arrived with Peter, completing the tally of climbers. They were sunburned and glowing. They had had a tremendous time, camping at 6600 metres on Baruntse and climbing to 6800 before being turned back by the avalanche conditions. Then they had opted for an unpleasant descent through the Barun Icefall, with frightening abseils. So all was well with us. Perhaps what Mingma had sensed was the impending tragedy just ten miles away on Lhotse, where Jerzy Kukuczka and Ryszard Pawlovski were building up to their summit bid on the unclimbed South Face.

Mingma's dream had found an echo in Andy. A recurrent night-mare haunted him too. It was about his descent from Chogolisa in 1986, when he left Hamish, Ulric and the others of his team. They were preparing the last bivouac, but Andy thought his toes were frost-bitten, and raced down to base in the dark. The next morning the team found Andy's tracks wandering across crevasses leaving black holes under his footprints. And the toes? They were fine after all. Now Andy's nightmare was telling him not to set foot on Makalu.

While we were setting up our camp a French team led by Pierre Béghin settled on the alluvial fan below us. Béghin planned to climb the Yugoslav route on the South Face of Makalu. This was probably the finest pure alpine-style route waiting to be done in the Himalaya. My opinion.

The French doctor, Michel, joined Andy, Ulric, Sustad and me for the afternoon. About fifty metres above our campsite was another terrace, littered with ten-metre granite boulders set in meadow grass. We had come here to do a bit of bouldering, "faire du bloc". The climb to the upper terrace took a breathless five minutes. It was at 5000 metres after all. But the bouldering was unsurpassed. We called this place Haut Fontainebleau.

Later we were joined by another Frenchman, Alain Gersain, who was a superb rock climber. So superb, in fact, that he was ranked tenth in the Grand Prix circuit, a real competitor. But according to Pierre, that was not much use: "Een ze eemalaya . . . zere ees no comparison. Rock climbing an mountaineering are like bicycling an football. Zey are not all ze same." Maybe not, but they do go together rather well, there can be no better foil to the brutal thuggery of high-altitude climbing than rock gymnastics.

"I guess this is the best bouldering I've ever seen," said Steve. "This place should be on the bouldering map of the world." Now that would be a good tour, I thought. Nepal, Thailand, Arizona, Paris, all that is best in bouldering, and not bad in food either. Except Arizona.

This was a "rest day". After the round of boulder problems, I washed my clothes, while Steve ("Washing is boring") read Richard Ellmann's biography of Oscar Wilde.

The entire team was at base, and after supper the hissing Tilley lamp cast a sharp shadowed light on the faces, while the conversation meandered like a relaxed shoal of red herrings. Rob said he'd rather not eat fish, his vegetarianism was against cruelty and killing. This led to toxic concentrations in shellfish (Gill), trout poaching in Ireland (Calvin), Norwegian fish recipes and the truth about crabsticks (Sustad, of course, who sat on his copy of Ellmann, just in case the conversation turned out to be boring). And finally, various methods of delousing fish farm trout. As I walked back to my tent I could still hear snippets from the mess tent. It was a windless night. The moon flittered through the shifting clouds, and candle-lit, the tents glowed on the black hillside.

Bruno and Ernst from the international Teutonophone (German, Austrian and Swiss) expedition arrived during breakfast. They had come down from their base at 5400 metres for a couple of days to re-acclimatise properly, and hoped to sleep in our mess tent. They had news of the outside world: Graf had won the tennis, and Prost the Formula One. I asked about the cricket, to loud and, I thought, very ignorant, guffaws from the American, Irish and Dutch members of our team.

The sight of the Teutonophones gave Steve one of his brilliant ideas: Bruno and Ernst could use our tents here, in exchange we would sleep at their camp on the way up to the Makalu La, kick-off point for an attempt on either Kangchungtse to the north, or the main challenge of the Makalu traverse to the south. The Teuton camp was a flowerless and grassless place, nestling in a barren fold of a lateral moraine opposite the stupendous West Pillar of Makalu, first climbed by Paragot's team in the seventies, later the scene of near-alpine-style ascents by John Roskelley and, in 1991, the amazing Kitty Calhoun. The star of this camp was undoubtedly Michl Dacher, fifty-six years old, and collecting his eleventh 8000-metre peak. Originally an electrician (like Kukuczka and Mike) from Munich, he turned professional five years ago.

A hundred metres and half an hour above Dacher's camp were the Catalans we had met on the road. Dacher had no time for them. The rate they were going they would "make the summit some time after Christmas". As for Béghin, what was the point of trying to climb a hard route when the chances of success were better on the normal route? Michl wanted to top out in the next two weeks then go home. So what were we doing? Acclimatising by doing surrounding peaks? Dacher looked baffled. "Does-not-compute!" registered in his eyes. So he reiterated for us, slowly so we could understand: "We come to climb Makalu I. We have not interest in Chago; we have not interest in Makalu II. We do not go left. We do not go right. We go to Makalu I.'

So logical. Although Sustad had espoused the study of chaos, it turned out that he knew a thing or two about German philosophy too. His unsuspected taste for Hegel and *Deutsch Idealismus* greatly impressed the Teutons. But not as much as when he produced his pee bottle. They'd never seen one before. Can pee bottles be an Anglophone invention? Can they be used as a philosophical argument? Could they refute one?

The Normal Route's Camp 1 (6200m) was another four-hour slog along the edge of the Chago Glacier, where a lone Teuton tent was outnumbered by a small village of tents from the other expeditions.

There was a collection of Catalan tents, infelicitously next to a group of Spanish Police tents, and soon there would be an American camp here too. The Catalans complained loudly, and to anyone who cared to listen, that the Spanish team were actually a "police team. They come from a little place near Catalonia; it is called Spain." Michl Dacher had his own view about the Latin quarter: "Ach, I cannot understand why they have so many tents at Camp 1. Such a *Stadt*! And no street signs!" But I was impressed by the Catalans: astute fund-raisers, they had sold Makalu by the metre, and given each sponsor a crate of sparkling wine with a "Vino Makalu" label.

Here at last it was possible to see the West Face which hangs out into space in the most disturbing manner. And one has to see it to understand the enormity of the enterprise that Kukuczka, Kurtyka and MacIntyre undertook in 1981. The central feature, the thing you cannot tear your eyes away from, is a blank granite wall from, I suppose, 7600 metres to 8300 metres. This makes it the same size as Half Dome. I have never seen snow settle on the face, so it is at least as steep as Half Dome. To reach the base of the granite wall you have to climb almost 2000 metres of steep ice, and then the difficulties begin.

This wall has been dubbed by climbing media as the next Great Problem, involving Yosemite-style big walling at 8000 metres. But think about it for a moment. Anyone can point to a wall and say, "That's the next problem". But what does this, the highest big wall in the world, really involve? The MacIntyre team climbed forty metres of the headwall before giving up. Since then more of the world's finest Himalayan specialists have gone to "have a look" and having seen, thought better of it. The problem is that no one is ready to climb this particular wall alpine-style yet. And to siege the wall,

Yosemite-style, at over 8000 metres, means spending not hours, but days and weeks, at that altitude. Roskelley and his team spent ten days in a continuous push on Uli Biaho in the Karakoram, on a wall, smaller, probably easier, and 2000 metres lower than Makalu. The West Wall would demand that kind of effort, but with a barometric pressure down to a quarter of that at sea level. You would require the big wall experience of a Roskelley (not many of those around), on top of which you would need supreme resistance to the altitude. The golden granite wall might look beautiful to the trekker, but to a climber it is brutal.

Such was the view through the shredded clouds. For the time being, the clouds also obscured the view we should have had of the West Face of Kangchungtse. The clouds heralded a snow fall, and twenty-four hours later Sustad and I were back in base.

The Great Disappearing Rice Rebellion had begun. Hamish, whose job was to monitor food stocks, found there was only one bag of rice left. The Sherpa staff threatened to walk out when we tried a Let-Them-Eat-Chapatis regime. They do eat rice three times a day, after all. It was all very difficult, no one knew what to do, everyone had their own explanation of what had gone wrong. I thought the staff looked overworked. Hamish thought it was all a mess. While Harriet, wearing the anthropologist's hat, said with a lopsided smile that it was "because Hamish had insulted them during their meal time; it breaks all their codes . . . Nati told me."

Peter and Harriet started filming close up. Perhaps here at last was the evidence needed. Scene: the climbers being utterly beastly to the Sherpas. Scene: climbers force Sherpas to eat unsavoury chapatis instead of wholesome rice. Scene: climber elbows film crew out of the way while maltreating Sherpas.

I was finding it hard to mediate with a wide-angle lens stuck up my nose. Mr Khanal calmly took me to one side. He spoke in a low voice, and made sense of the puzzle. The missing piece of the jigsaw was Nati. The reason we were so short of rice was that half our rice stocks had disappeared during the walk-in and the kitchen staff blamed Nati. As a sirdar he had been ineffectual, the organisation of the porters had been left to Lapka Dorji and the Pasang. Yet we had hired Nati because on Mike and Lindsay's previous expedition, to Annapurna III, he had proved a clever and hard-working helper for Lapka-the-Cook. Perhaps Nati had not shown sufficient tact now he was nominally in charge of Lapka.

This was the point at which Mr Khanal showed that behind his golden smile lay a diplomat's brain. Somehow Mr Khanal persuaded Nati to apologise to the others. We all hugged each other. Hamish in a fit of pure relief turned to the wide-angle lens under his elbow and said, "Go away" or words to that effect. But to solve the real problem Hamish sent a message to Shedowa, six days away, for two more bags of rice; though that is not the way the film crew saw it.

Our next attempt to reach the Makalu La illustrated some of the problems found on so-called "normal" routes on 8000-metre mountains. We had moved our minuscule tent up to 6600 metres, next to the Teutonophone Camp 2, some way below the Catalan Camp 2 at 6800 metres. We found the Catalans had laid fixed rope out on the slope below their Camp 2, which was so gentle we could only assume the rope had been fixed in case of avalanche. Certainly using it could only slow one down. But Rob and Nati had had a bust-up with the Catalans the day before, who said: "We make the way, we put in the markers, we fix the rope . . . You cannot use our rope . . . You must find another way."

I had heard about this sort of thing, that on some mountains the teams actually sell on their fixed gear to following expeditions. Sustad and I were prepared for cross words when we reached the Catalan tents, but were greeted with . . . tea. And smiles.

"It's the Latin temperament," said Sustad. "Real difficult to predict." I wondered what the Catalans think of prejudiced American-Scandinavians. More to the point, we had taken care not to touch their ropes at all. We pushed on, to about 7000 metres, before turning round. It was 10 a.m. The long uphill plod was boring, and we'd done enough to justify going on to the next stage of the sports plan.

We had also now had a closer look at the West Face of Kangchungtse. There was definitely a line, right up the middle of the face. We had scanned the glacier below the face for, and found, tell-tale signs of loose stones. Then again there were the séracs on the right of the face. How safe it was, we could not agree, but technically there certainly seemed to be a line.

Just about everyone else was back in base now. Andy and Ulric had a magnificent time on Peak 4, making a three-day first ascent of the jagged mountain. Mike and Lindsay had returned from a protracted exploration of the Pethangtse region. We'd long since given up trying to elicit any information more detailed than that from those two.

Nati arrived at base shortly afterwards. He was not alone. He had been down to the local hermitage of Neh Karta and married the hermit's daughter. It turned out that the hermit was also Hamish's Banana Lama.

"Make sense of that one if you can," said Stephen.

Nati was dressed as nattily as ever with dark glasses and new climbing boots, a real Sherpani's man. His new wife retired shyly to the kitchen tent, where she was immediately dubbed the Banana Lassi by Hamish. With them was Kevin Brubaski, a photographer who had a wonderful eye and fluent Nepali. He was to help Peter and Harriet with the camera work and translate for them. Kevin was interested in everything that moved, and soon discovered that Mingma's ghost was a reincarnation of the Sherpa who died during Edmund Hillary's Makalu reconnaissance of 1954.

Having wintered under Ama Dablam, Hillary's party had brought Solo Khumbu Sherpas with them and crossed from the Khumbu to Barun by way of West Col at 6135 metres and another col at 6110 metres to their camp site, the first grass they found, about a kilometre up valley of our base. The story goes that when the Sherpa died, his parents came to fetch the body, and the col at 6110 metres took its name, Sherpani Col, from his mother. The Banana Lama told Kevin that Solo Khumbu Sherpas should not be in Barun, and by staying here had invited bad karma.

Mingma's dreams had returned, so he had decided to go home to Kathmandu. "Perhaps he has a beautiful wife," said Steve. As for Andy, he had thoroughly enjoyed Peak 4, and now he had had enough. He'd trek home with Mingma. They reinforced each other's dreams. Andy said, "If I stay, I'll only want to climb Makalu, and I don't want to do that."

No one criticised Andy. The decision to go required great strength, and was harder, really, than deciding to stay with us. It was a sad day. We loved Andy for his ridiculous and sometimes blind enthusiasms. And yet, in one sense, I envied him, stepping back into the light, while we would have to remain in limbo. Andy had one last afternoon at Haut Fontainebleau with us. It was cold, the wind blew clouds across the face of the sun. But we threw ourselves into the chain of problems, punching up this overhang, creeping across that slab, arm twisters, finger rippers, contorted mantles; chess for the body. It was a celebration, a sort of reverse wake.

It was now late September. At base the tail-end of the monsoon was still producing evening downpours. The heavy rain drummed on the mess tent. Annette pattered in competition on the portable typewriter. Stephen and I were stuffing ourselves with peanut butter and broken biscuits. Rob said he was now going to climb the normal route.

"I just want to make a safe and efficient ascent of Makalu. This will be my last and only chance to climb an 8000-metre peak. I've promised myself and my family that I would not try another. I want to see if I can manage it."

Hamish and Ulric too had opted for the normal route. Which left Steve and me packed and ready for the next stage of our plan.

Chapter Five

Kangchungtse

Kangchungtse lies north of the Makalu La, and was first climbed in the autumn of 1954 by Jean Franco, Lionel Terray, Gyaltsen Norbu and Pa Norbu. The first ascensionists followed what was to become the Normal Route to Makalu I as far as the Makalu La, they then climbed the short South Face of Kangchungtse directly to the summit ridge. Steve's researches revealed only one other route to the summit, the fine North Ridge, by S. Nara and Lhapka Norbu in 1976. There had been a number of attempts on the West Face, which all seemed to have been repulsed by stonefall.

The West Face of Kangchungtse was a natural secondary objective for the expedition. It looked like typical TD country, about 1000 metres high, with a central snowfield, a rim of summit cliffs, and granite slabs seamed with ice gullies in the lower half. The left side of the face had big black and red cliffs, from which we supposed the stonefall emanated. The right flank was guarded by a large sérac. There was a possible line through the mixed ground, a faint depression slanting from the bottom right corner up to a narrow gully in the centre of the face. We had watched the face, and noted that the sun reached the central section soon after 9.00 a.m. We reasoned that if only we could pass the centre of the face before 9.30 a.m. we should avoid the worst of any stonefall. That was about as much as Steve and I could agree on. Where to bivouac, how much gear to take, who would take the tent, whether to add bivibags to the sleeping bags, what food and gas . . . all these things became so controversial that we gave up the idea of a so-called alpine-style ascent altogether. We would not take any of it. Just a water-bottle each. Sort of Scottish-style, I suppose. Five Russian ice screws, half a dozen pegs, a 9 mm and a

7 mm rope, a few slings. We should have a pretty good chance of returning to our tent the same day. Or so we thought.

My alarm watch blittered dutifully at midnight, I turned it off and went back to sleep. An hour later, pricked with guilt, I wriggled out of the sleeping bag, cursed the snowstorm of condensation, and unzipped the entrance. It is a unique property of our tent that the entrance is designed for dwarves. Anyone fractionally larger than a midget has to belly-crawl through the frozen soup and discarded noodles that always collect at tent entrances. These tents also have something called a valance, designed to catch snow and dump it down your neck as you emerge. This time the valance also grabbed my headtorch. It made me gargle with rage, neckfuls of snow, frozen soup, noodles, and somewhere in the icy mess was my torch. I was still half asleep. Normally this was sufficient excuse to abandon the tent. Here was the moment of chaological instability. Had it not been for the neck trap, a chaologist might argue, Steve and I would have slept peacefully till dawn, then walked down to base in time for lunch and an afternoon kip. Instead, by one o'clock that night, we were plodding up towards the bergschrund, following the track we had made the evening before. It was 6500 metres. It was dark. There was no moon. Like an evil shadow, the West Face blotted out the stars. The only noise was the shuffle of our snow-shoes, and my asthmatic wheezing as I struggled to keep up with Steve.

A fragile bridge crossed the bergschrund, above which we untied the ropes, trailing them behind. My rope only stuck among the rocks once, Steve's jammed whenever I trod on it. Immediately above the bergschrund the climbing was easy, low-angle ice ribbons weaving between granite outcrops. Our main problem was to pick the continuous line. This was done by switching off the torches and peering at the dark until the faintly luminescent ice appeared to glow around the buttresses. By 5.00 a.m. we reached the end of the ice ribbons. There were rock walls to negotiate, usually by steep ice bulges, or hidden ramps and grooves. Soon the climbing became quite technical, we needed to see to find the route, and where to place runners, so we were pretty self-satisfied when, just as we needed it to, the sky lightened. So far things were going to plan. Two pitches later we witnessed dawn flooding the Kangshung Face of Everest and Lhotse Shar. A sea of cloud filled the Barun valley below us, lapping against the islands of Chamlang, Baruntse, and Tutse. In every climb there is a moment when it all seems worth while, and dawn on Kangchungtse was our moment. It lasted about ten minutes. Then the constant front pointing began to hurt. The ice was wintry, hard and glassy. Axes and points teetered on half-sunk placements, and it became important to gain that central gully before the stones came rattling down the face.

Steve led a pitch up and left out of the Spider, an Eiger-like feature we had identified during the process of writing our route description, estimating the pitches and time required, and setting down compass bearings for the descent. All of this was supposed to aid us in case of bad weather. (Its real purpose was to divert our thoughts from the consequences of coming unstuck.) Down and to the left again lay the entry to the steep gully. It sported vertical ice steps, brittle stalactites, capped with powdery cornices, so we climbed a buttress to the left. At least there we could find fine spike runners. By 1.30 p.m. we reached the large central névé. Our difficulties should have been over, but the snow was thigh-deep and had been softened deep below the surface by raw, high-altitude sun. The original plan had been to climb to the main summit by a series of linked snowfields, but now we could barely move. In one hour we plodded no more than 100 metres, so we chose a line that exited through the summit cliffs to the right of the main summit.

The perfect weather of the morning began to deteriorate through the afternoon. By 3.00 p.m. we were only able to spot our route through intermittent clearings. We were aiming for a vertical chimney, blocked with a blank-looking boulder, which appeared to lead onto a couple of pitches of slanting snow ramps. We reached the Chimney Pitch at 5.00 p.m. The next two pitches were the hardest of the day. First there was a little gentle rock climbing, swinging about on a poorly frozen-in spike, then in order to avoid doing anything too intimate with the jammed boulder, I followed a friendly-looking but deceitful corner filled with ice. The filling fell out about half-way up. It wasn't much good anyway, the red rock grinned through, giving it an unsettling pink sort of colour; nor was the filling concealing any ledges or cracks. Not long after the ice fell out of the corner, I noted my last runner was too far away. The corner ended with a blank wall, and still no runner. There was another groove over to the right. It was a long stride. Wheezing a little, I watched a trembling leg stretch out towards the groove. The body, also trembling, followed the step, then a delicate traverse across thinly iced slabs and, thankfully, to a patch of snow. It was darkening quickly. Belaying took ages, the cracks were blind. The only usable flake was loose. I placed a couple of pegs behind the loose flake, and dug a small stance.

When Steve followed, it was without a headtorch, groping for the ice. We thought we had cracked it. Only snow ramps above. But again we had been misled by the snow. Steve's pitch was a horror show. It was on 60-degree granular powder, like a hill of salt. The snow was waist deep generally, but would occasionally become much deeper, and then Steve had to struggle to make any kind of progress. He sank deeper with each effort to move up. The deepest powder lay below rock steps, which he had to mantel-shelf, having first cleared a vertical trench. There were no runners, of course. In the dark, I saw none of this. All I knew was that I was shivering on the stance. I was cold. I wanted out. I shouted things I ought not have. But when my turn came, I understood why I had been left freezing for two hours.

A couple of slightly easier pitches led to the summit ridge. It was 9.30 p.m., completely dark, and blowing a snowstorm. We had arrived at the point marked 7600 metres on the excellent Schneider map, a sort of South Summit. Turning left would, we knew, in so far as we knew anything, take us to the main summit forty metres higher. Turning right would take us down. We turned right.

It cannot be said that we lost our way coming down, we never knew it. The map showed the Makalu La as being due south. It did not show the bands of cliffs across the face. We had no idea of their existence until we almost fell over them. Heading due south, we moved roped together, first down a knife-edge with a cornice undercutting it, then a broad gully. Steve slipped down a powder-filled chimney which looked like an innocuous snow gully, but the snow fell away as he stepped into the chimney and left him dangling. Below the chimney the slope was cut across by a blackness which swallowed the torch light. In tiredness and despondency we turned to the left, and followed the edge of this thing, long cliff or enormous bergschrund, we could not tell what. After a while we found ourselves confronted with a broad easy ice ramp which cut across the black thing and led us down to the plateau of the Makalu La.

The next part of our story is a little confused. We were tired, hungry, and the water in our bottles had frozen. Ice berries formed in jangling bunches on our moustaches and, though irritating at first, later proved a useful source of water when licked.

We needed to follow compass bearings. But facing into the storm, which blew from the south, was unpleasant. So we measured the wind direction, and walked into it. Whenever I put the damn compass into my pocket, the wind changed direction; it must have, because twice we checked our bearings only to find we were heading north, away from the Makalu La. My brains had become quite addled. I remember saying to myself that I really did not want to go down Five Finger or the Steall Gully again, as I had done so often before. Trying hard, I managed to recall the consequences of descending the wrong way off the Makalu La. It would take us down to the Kangshung Glacier, via the séracs of Chomo Lonzo. We would finish up in Tibet, and we did not have our passports.

After the second balls-up, Steve turned to me, and relieved himself of a great outpouring of spleen, which I would guess were mostly unprintable Americanisms, but the friendly gale took the words away before I could hear. I gave him the compass. We plodded on, knee deep, thankful for the snow-shoes, the compass-bearer shouting directions to the trail-breaker, but all I could hear was the wind. By 2.30 a.m. Steve's toes had begun to freeze and he needed to loosen his boots. Also, we were a little lost. Perhaps dawn might bring new information. Our bivouac was a pair of holes in the snow. The idea had been to dig deep enough to get out of the wind, throw the rucksack into the bottom, and sit out the night, but the rucksacks filled the holes and projected us back into the weather. Steve slept well, his head thrown back, muttering peacefully. I spent the time shaking with cold and cursing the frozen water while trying to melt the chips of ice by breathing into the neck of the bottle. Five a.m. brought light, clouds and more snow, and that familiar conversation:

"Have you got the compass?"

"No, I gave it to you."

"I don't think so . . ."

We just looked at each other.

"Perhaps I put it down beside me . . ." Steve began to sift through the powder, but it was no use. An arm's depth of snow had fallen in the night.

"Let's wait." We had no choice. "Perhaps there will be a gap in the clouds." There was no arguing with that.

After an hour, a dim outline which we guessed to be Kangchungtse gave us a rough bearing. Keeping the full fifty metres of rope stretched out, we managed to steer a straightish line till we stumbled on the three empty tents of the Catalan Camp 3, and knew that we had joined the Normal Route again. The tents were at 7500 metres, we had overshot the La and were now on our way up Makalu. Somewhere below us were drifted-over tracks leading to fixed ropes and Camp 2. Stumbling and down climbing, slowly sensing that we were losing height, we passed down buttresses, broad gullies and avalanche slopes. We became involved in one small avalanche, it took us fifty metres further on our way. Steve's only comment, brushing the snow-dust out of his hat, was, "I hate avalanches . . ."

By late afternoon we began to recognise the contours, the séracs, and the shape of the slots. I shouted to Steve that our tent had gone. Then I realised that it was the small pyramid of fresh snow a few metres away. We had been away just forty-six hours, and in that time over a metre of snow had fallen. It had taken all day to reach our tent.

The next day, still dehydrated enough to produce dark brown pee, we packed the tent, sleeping bags, stove and our rubbish. The rucksacks were heavy, and the snow feathery. When we sat down, the sacks dragged us below the surface. The descent to 6000 metres should have taken an hour. It took five. In the blank whiteness, wheezing and gasping under the squeeze of the monstrous loads, we waited for clear patches to drift our way. Then one of the Catalan marker flags would appear briefly. To fix the direction before the flag disappeared, one of us would hurl a ski stick in the right direction. It was a halting procession. In one place, where the way lay down the steep side of a sérac, a hissing noise came out of the snow as I stepped on it, and then as if a knife had been drawn across it, a slice opened across the slope. Shaking with fear I drew my foot back. I suddenly felt sick, and sat down, forgetting about the feathery snow.

"What's it like?" asked Steve, addressing a pair of boots sticking out of a hole in the snow.

"I think we might be stuck," I muttered, trying to clear my face and glasses of snow.

The problem was that the only way down was this slope, bivouacking there was uninviting, and uphill retreat unthinkable. The solution was a small crevasse above the slope, and the job of belaying from inside the crevasse fell to me. I tied the two ropes together to lower Steve, whose job was to set off the avalanche by descending in the clumsiest way possible. The task was just up his street, and soon he had set off a magnificent chest-deep slab, which took the entire slope before it. Unfortunately he lost his way in the whiteness, and had to traverse the vertical face of a sérac, front pointing his snow-shoes, to regain an avalanche cone which crossed the last crevasse, before supper. We had had enough of such novelties by the time we reached the deserted tented village of Camp 1.

Chapter Six

Back to Kathmandu

At the Teuton Camp, there was sweet black tea and a warm welcome. Michl Dacher hugged us like prodigal sons. "I thought you were lost! I thought you were lost! I am so happy to see you, I looked with glasses, maybe a track here – or there! But my eyes are not so good. Maybe there is Stephen, or Victor but I do not see them. I am so happy!" Actually so were we. We'd come to like and respect this eccentric German who, it seemed, would be finishing off the last of his 8000-metre peaks in his retirement. His tent had salamis and hams dangling like a delicatessen. He would eat nothing that was not wholesome and natural. Sausage, boiled potatoes, cabbage and rice. He would not touch dehydrated stuff.

"Food in packets? It is not possible climb if you eat powder! Man must eat food. This is food!" He held out a potato for us to examine.

"What is it for?" asked Steve.

"Dunno," I said, "never seen nuffink like it before."

The next ten miles had been bare rocks, boulders and scree when we went up. Now the snow was so deep and soft, we needed to wear snow-shoes all the way to base, arriving just after dark, at eight o'clock, and finding it under a metre of snow. Some kind soul had dug out our tents regularly to stop them collapsing, and canyon-like paths had been excavated between the tents.

Kees, still whiffing slightly of mushrooms, produced Dutch cigars. We puffed at the cigars and sipped mugs of strong sweet coffee, feeling rather pleased with our effort. I said to Rob, "At least we got up one of our objectives, eh?" But Rob took the opportunity to give me a lecture. "You and Steve were wrong to do it. I wouldn't

have gone up. You only got away with it because you were lucky."
About an hour later I thought of a suitably pithy reply. There should
be a name for it, finding the rejoinder when it is far too late. What
is the opposite of riposte?

Stephen's toes had not turned black, but they hurt and he needed
morphiates at night, and Gill advised him not to climb for a while.
Once damaged, the toes were more susceptible to serious frostbite.
So he was off back to Haringey.

One morning Kees woke to find a tiny yellow tent had been
pitched near his. It was Kazuo, who became a satellite of our
base. Kazuo Kawakami was Japanese, of course. The night Stephen
decided to leave, our home-brew beer barrel was declared "fit" for
drinking by Hamish and Ulric. The barrel was meant to hold about
eighty litres, and by midnight it was empty. Kazuo had been silent
for a while; no one had noticed exactly when he stopped speaking.
He was sitting bolt upright, but now he failed to respond to any
questions. Someone reached out and pushed him gently. Slowly
and gracefully, like a vertically challenged caber, Kazuo toppled.
And lay perfectly still. Gill helped him up, jammed his headtorch
on his head, and pointed him at the door.

The conversation ran on till someone saw a light flashing outside
the mess. Calvin peered out, and told us, "Itsh a shearchlight! Sho
it ish."

We all staggered to our feet to see Kazuo, spinning round and
round, wondering which direction his tent had gone in.

When he arrived at our camp, Kazuo had given Nati 2000 rupees
for Lapka Dorji to purchase an air ticket from Tumlintar, but Nati had
passed only 1000 rupees on to Lapka Dorji, who returned the money
to Kazuo two weeks later because the flights were fully booked.

Because Kazuo spoke English rather badly, Nati was able to
contradict him flatly when he complained, "Me, Nati two-oh-oh-oh.
Two thousand!"

"He only give me 1000 rupees. He is stupid, he mean one
thousand. He cannot speak English."

"Me to Nati, two thousand," insisted Kazuo.

No one knew whom to believe till Lapka Dorji reappeared and
forced Nati to return the balance of the cash.

Kazuo wanted to reach the Makalu La, solo. He had a permit for
the summit the following year, and this was his reconnaissance. Gill
and Hamish, Rob and Calvin were going on to the Normal Route
in pairs. Ulric looked like mounting a solo attempt on Makalu, by

the same route. Mike and Lindsay were, as usual, inscrutable. I was exhausted, and needed a rest. The plans for the traverse of Makalu had departed with Sustad.

By early October, our remaining active climbers were at Camp 1 or higher. Peter had joined the climbers and sent back his Aaton in order to make a summit bid unencumbered with cameras. There were now no less than thirty people trying to get up the Normal Route, members of the American, British, Spanish, Teutonophone and Catalan expeditions.

Only the French remained out of the Normal arena as a means of ascent. Pierre Béghin reached the summit in the afternoon of the 6th, after a remarkable ascent of the South Face. From the end of his fixed ropes, at 7000 metres, he had climbed alone for three days. His effort was in the league of the very finest Himalayan ascents. His descent from the summit was not quite so controlled. He climbed down the Normal Route, and became involved in a 200-metre avalanche, which landed him by the entrance to a Catalan tent. The following day a 400-metre avalanche stripped him of his rucksack and ice axe. All grist to the mill: Béghin worked in Grenoble as an avalanche scientist. He was by now very ill, coughing and in need of antibiotics. In hard climbs at high altitude, the body's defences crumble very quickly, and even with the strongest mountaineers, climbing is a race against a physiological time bomb. Pierre escaped from the mountain just in time.

Calvin and Mike returned from Makalu shortly after Béghin. They had retreated because of the windslab.

"We saw Michl Dacher dangling on the fixed ropes like a fish. All the slope around him going down. But Rob's still going up. They're all obsessed, it's madness." Mike pointed at his head, so I put a large mug of tea in his hands.

Calvin said, "Béghin's used up all the luck on the hill for the year."

The winter winds set in soon after this. The summit ridges of Makalu sounded like a jet engine revving up. The temperature dropped several degrees. The monsoon had ended abruptly, but the clear skies following the rain had brought the jet stream. The window of opportunity had hardly opened before firmly shutting again and almost closing on Béghin. No other ascents of the mountain were completed that autumn.

Singly and in pairs, the others returned from the mountain. It was time to go. Nati's temporary wife, having practised traditional Sherpa polyandry, decided to return to the hermitage.

Two weeks later we were in the Tibet Guest House again. Back in the Great Flesh Pot. Here Mike paid off our Base Camp staff with large bonuses to all except Nati who left the room muttering dire threats. Later, he would be visited by the film team.

The other expeditions were in town, too, waiting for their flights to ferry them home. The Catalans showed us a place that had "real *cappuccino*", and gave us news of the Polish disaster on Lhotse. The leader, Jerzy Kukuczka, had been killed.

When the Poles returned, Ryszard Pawlovski, who had been Kukuczka's climbing partner, told us the story. October 24th was to have been their summit day. They had reached 8300 metres on mixed ground, and were using 6 mm rope bought second hand from a Korean expedition. The Poles had already seen one instance of this rope breaking. At 9.00 a.m. on the first pitch after the bivouac Kukuczka ran out thirty metres and appeared to have reached some kind of final cornice. Ryszard saw his arms flailing in the snow, then Jerzy began to slide, then tumble. He fell past Ryszard, past the bivouac ledge and out into overhanging space. "He had no chance, he was flying fifty metres." The rope snapped, and his body was found two days later at 5400 metres, where he was given a crevasse burial. It took Ryszard the rest of the day to descend 250 metres to Camp 6, the top of the fixed ropes. He arrived in the dark with no headtorch. Three days later Ryszard reached base. His weary eyes were empty as he told me how the day before the summit attempt Kukuczka's wife had contacted the Polish team by radio, and had begged Jerzy to come home.

Kukuczka was the second man to climb all the 8000-metre peaks. But he had added to the task by making new routes or winter ascents of all except Lhotse, which had been his first 8000-metre peak and the only one he had climbed by the normal route, in summer. Achieving the South Face would have finally completed his exotic set of routes.

Up to 1988, there were something like a dozen climbers who had climbed more than four 8000-metre peaks, and none of them had died in the high mountains. Perhaps there was a learning curve, perhaps it gets safer, we thought, once you learn to cope with the risks. Then there was Marcel Ruedi, who had climbed ten of the fourteen peaks. He collapsed and died on Makalu in 1986. He had been out of Geneva just thirteen days when he died. Since that time the statistics have changed. Now, of the list of those who have climbed more than four 8000ers, about a quarter are no longer alive. Years ago René Desmaison summed it up: "The mountain does not know you are an expert."

Yet to me, and most of the people I met in those days, Kukuczka's death was unbelievable. How could the greatest exponent of Himalayan climbing, a man whose strength and skill had protected him like a charm, be only mortal after all?

In the Old Vienna, Mike and I found Michl Dacher and his friend Bruno Zaug. They were wearing Sih Stones, Tibetan charms, round their necks. Michl had been given his by Messner. Mike examined Bruno's white macaroni-shaped tube. It was seamed with black markings like symmetrical eyes. "They don't know how it is made, maybe insects. They are thousands of years old, and they put them on dead lamas for the next life."

"Did you know that Kukuczka was also given one?" Dacher said.

"Was he wearing it when he fell?"

"They say he was not."

Chapter Seven

London, Spring 1990

"It might have started in the pub. Most expeditions do. Maybe a chance mention of the mountain led to a beery response. Perhaps this led in turn to increasing enthusiasm, or a position difficult to back down from. One never remembers the details. Suddenly there is an expedition. Expeditions are like the full frontal storms of recent years, no one really knows how or where they start. On a South Pacific island a butterfly flaps its wings in a particular way . . ."

Dark coffee rings decorated a sheaf of typesheets. I couldn't concentrate on the writing. My brain hurt. I had betrayed my age by playing John Wesley Harding, turned up to the max. The dull throbbing inside my head was now overlain by a repeated ringing. No, no, that ringing was the phone. It was Sustad. He had a problem to show me.

Dark and drizzling. The wiper blades smeared the London grease across the screen, making it necessary to lean forward and peer through the one patch the wipers had missed. Old Ford roundabout. Hadn't driven a car for three months, felt strange. Burdett Road. Wet tarmac, straight on at the lights, left past the dismally wet, and never used, games park, into Cordova Road. The car rumbled as if it was falling apart. Ah yes, I forgot, Cordova Road is cobbled. Sharp left at the sinister industrial tower, slide on the wet cobbles, three Alsatians from hell snarled through the wire of XXX Security. Red muddy gravel squeaked under the driving wheels, as I parked the car by the sign of the North London Rescue Commando. A bizarre name for the Mile End Climbing Wall.

Richard, white haired, looking no older than last spring, looked
up as I paid my pound.

"Haven't seen you for a while, where have you been hiding?"

"Nepal."

The soles of the feet felt cold on the concrete as I changed
from trainers to slippers. Inside my stomach was a small knot of
anticipation. I felt like that man in *Metamorphosis* who wakes up
as a beetle. Only after expeditions I wake up as a beginner. The
arms looked skinny. Well, it *was* the first attempt to use them for
four months.

Steve was already there, he showed me the problem – there were
two very small lumps like a pair of eyebrows on this overhanging
wall. Above was a tiny edge sloping sideways. You got two fingers
on the edge, and rocked up onto your toes on one of the eyebrows.
You were off balance, and had to move through this position quickly,
or fall off. If you could slide through fast enough, you'd have the
momentum to leap for a small pocket, just out of reach. I groaned
with frustration. Burnt off by Steve, *and* he was handicapped. He
couldn't do up the laces on one foot. Frostbite. But I just couldn't
slap my hand anywhere near the pocket. "The brute's taller than
me," I consoled myself. We turned to another problem, three
head-sized lumps of artificial rock; you had to stand on your hand,
pulling your fingers out from under the foot, wedging your left foot
against the wall, push up and grab the third block. This time, I
chanced on the right set of movements and retained balance. Steve
was a shade too tall. The geometry didn't work for him. Besides
which, Steve has a forehead like a dolphin, and I am sure it puts
him off balance.

"Cheers!" Our first since getting back. I handed him the coffee-
stained typescript and leant back on the upholstered bench to watch
my friend while he read. Across the glistening table he sipped beer
with a chalk-dusted hand, his tee shirt looked trashed and his jeans
torn dirty with work. The huge forehead was brown and elongated
by the beer glass. After a while he looked up and said:

"Easter Island?"

"Pitcairn?" I suggested.

"I bet it was Vairaatea."

"No, no, no. Hereheretue, for sure."

"Naw, it probably all started in the pub."

PART TWO

ULTAR

1991

The Karakoram forms the western wing of the great Himalayan chain. It is easy to be superlative about the range: it contains the greatest concentration of high peaks in the world and the greatest area of glaciation outside the Poles. But the real attraction is the sheer beauty of the granite spires. The majority of expeditions visit only a few selected valleys. For example, in 1991 there were some fifty expeditions to the Karakoram of which seventy per cent attempted to climb just six popular peaks. As a direct result of this concentration, there are still magnificent opportunities for exploration in the range. Ultar was one such opportunity. At 7388 metres (24,239 feet), this was, at the time of our expedition, one of the highest unclimbed peaks in the range, rather surprising considering the peak is less than five kilometres from the nearest road. But the Karakoram Highway is also five kilometres lower than the summit. There is no easy line, and any route to the summit from the south side would involve a climb of not less than 3500 metres from bergschrund to final cornice.

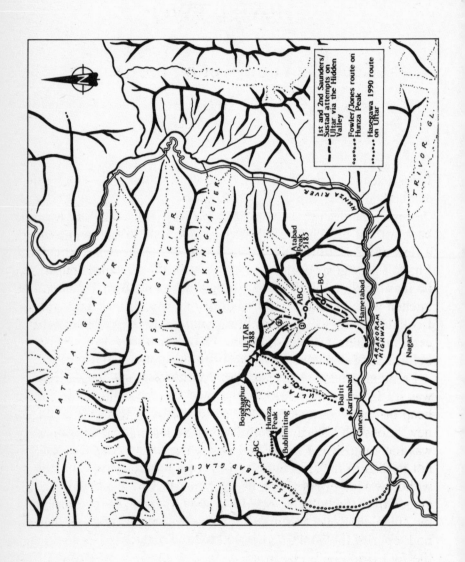

Chapter Eight

Keeping Your Feet on the Ceiling

I was excited. I had been sorting slides of Spantik, which I had climbed in 1987, but it was difficult to tell the quality through the small hand lens, so I began to project the mountains onto the back wall of the kitchen. There was one slide I kept returning to, a view of the Batura Wall from Spantik. There was something there I hadn't previously noticed. A tower, yes, I'd seen that before. But no feasible route to it had been apparent. Now, projected onto the kitchen wall, there was a line leading to the tower. A ridge or spur, I couldn't exactly decide what the photograph was telling me. But certainly, there was a possibility of a route where none had been before. Suddenly the tower became interesting.

I remembered having seen a similar view somewhere else. Where was it? In the attic? The stacked books in the living room? That heap of books in my study that always challenged me to build the new bookshelf? Because the thought of sorting through the heap was too repulsive, I knew that was where it must be. The trick is not to disturb the structural stability of a heap like that. I carefully withdrew a large, poorly printed volume, leaving the rest of the pile arched over the hole: *Polskie Wyprrawy Karakorum Alpinistycyzne* by Zbigniew Kowalewski and Andrzej Paczkowski. I gave a smug nod, opened the book, and there it was, a double-page spread with the fold irritatingly obscuring the centre of the tower. But it was there to be seen. A fantastic objective, unnoticed by everyone to date. What a secret. I felt like King Midas. I had to tell somebody or my ears would fall off . . . I rang Sustad and left him a message to meet me at Mile End in the evening. Next I rang Fowler, and he wasn't in either. I left the house for a run round our dismal

Islington block, but after a few minutes I developed an asthmatic
wheeze and had to walk home. I'd forgotten that I don't run without
my inhaler.

Sustad fell off in an explosion of chalk dust. Now it was my turn.
The first hold is the proverbial jug handle, the next is scalloped like
a shell. Your fingers seek out the hollow in its back. The third is the
shape of a cricket ball. It needs the sort of tight grip that leaves you
with aching forearms the next day. The holds are huge, so why does
it hurt so much? Because you are clinging to a completely horizontal
surface from the underside. You are trying to crawl across a ceiling
over two metres from the vinyl-covered foam mattresses. This is the
Pump Room, where stomach muscles tear at incipient hernia lines
as you raise your feet above your head. Here the holds pull away
from you with all the power of your own weight. There was one
particular combination our friend Ed Douglas could use to swing
across the entire six metres of the ceiling in five tarzanian swoops.
But surely this was cheating? Where is the fun in life if you don't
keep your feet on the ceiling?

Andy Reid had built the Mile End Wall piecemeal. It started
as a small traversing wall in a shed, then took over the adjacent
wall, and grew in height from two and a half metres to four and a
half. It began to sprout panels, plywood bolted to metal frames and
dotted with the new resin holds. The new holds were even better
than real rock, epoxy resin moulded to look like handy-sized bits
of dog dirt. Every time I came back from an expedition the wall had
grown. Longer. Bigger. Bizarrer. When I returned from Makalu,
an eight-metre steel frame had suddenly erected itself in the main
hall. Was the Mile End Wall's creator fighting a losing battle with a
Frankenstein's monster? The Pump Room was the Mad Scientist's
latest brainchild.

Steve pulled on a tee shirt, and looked on in disgust at the
crewcut, bulging-bodied young climbers cruising back and forth
across the ceiling, dangling from fingertips, enveloped in chalk,
mist.

"Come on, Victor, this is depressing. I know a better way of
exercising those arm muscles."

The Palmtree is a Victorian pub, isolated by the Luftwaffe in what
passes in Tower Hamlets for parkland. There is a bomb-damaged
terrace reaching out towards the pub. It doesn't make it. Inside, the
island bar spreads the public room out into a horseshoe. Steve likes

pubs and tells me they are the only lasting contribution to culture that the British have made.

He passed me my pint of Tolly, his hands still covered in chalk, as were his clothes and hair. Peering at me through chalk-blurred National Health frame glasses, he asked the question:

"OK. What is it?"

"It's this." I put the Polish book on the scratched oak table, brought out the slides I had taken from Spantik, and passed him the viewer. He gazed at the slides, then at the book, then back again as I explained the project.

"You see, I didn't think there was a safe way of getting to the tower, till I noticed that this slide shows a ridge going all the way down. You can see it here. It is *huge*. That glacier is at about 4000 metres, see? The top is 7388 metres. But it looks safe."

"And it's beautiful."

"Yes."

"When are we going?" He hadn't even bothered to ask its name.

The mountain that began to fill my waking hours with dreams was Ultar, at 7388 metres (approximately 24,000 feet) one of the highest unclimbed mountains in the world. But that fact was an irrelevance. Shape is more important than size. And this was one of the most shapely piles I had ever seen. Steve and I began to research the project. It rose out of the Hunza valley. It was virtually on the Karakoram Highway, the close neighbour of Bojohaghur, which I had spent so long on in 1984. Steve had been to the same area in 1985 with Doug Scott. We started writing to possible authorities, and first of all to Nazir Sabir. The first Pakistani climber to stand on the summit of K2 is not only a Hunza man, his father lived under the shadow of Ultar. He told us of the previous Japanese and Polish expeditions.

We also noticed there seemed to be a large part of Ultar hidden from the road. The bit we were interested in seemed to be in this invisible sector.

To understand the topography of Ultar it is best to consider the mountain as the junction of three arêtes. The highest of these comes from the north-west, from Bojohaghur. This arête is probably over 7300 metres all the way from Bojohaghur to Ultar, a distance of a mile or so. The next arête forms another high-level ridge and runs out to the east. This feature maintains a crest around the 7000-metre level. Finally there is a ridge falling more steeply due south. Of the three faces between these ridges, the South-West Face debouches into the Ultar nullah, the much visited deep gorge above Baltit fort and Karimabad; the North Face, above the Ghulkin and Gulmit Glaciers, can be seen spectacularly from Pasu and Batura on the Karakoram Highway; and there's the South-East Face which no one, not even Nazir Sabir, seemed to know anything about. Our photographs from Spantik showed a bowl of glaciers between the East and the South Ridges which the maps showed as a seven-fingered hand. Satellite photographs which I had found in the Map Room of the British Museum showed the same features. The map was not lying, though on the ground this entire glacier system was obscured by the outlying peaklets and subsidiary ridges of the mountain. There was nothing in the literature about this complex high valley system. You could drive the Karakoram Highway from Hunza for twenty miles to Pasu, past all three major facets, and still only see the South-West Face and the North Face. You could have driven three-quarters of the way round Ultar, and never suspected you had passed right under one of the major walls of the region, the 3500-metre Hidden South-East Face of Ultar. And the centre of that wall was the object we had seen from Spantik, the giant Hidden Pillar.

We started to think about possible additions to the team. Mick Fowler, who had been with me on Bojohaghur, was not sure about returning to the same area. "There is so much to see in the world, Vic," he protested. Steve had spent some time on the North-East Ridge of Everest with the Austrian climber and film-maker Robert Schauer, and wanted him to join us. Robert could only come if there was to be a film to fund his costs. So we brought in Kees t'Hooft again. Kees was a distant descendant of Jenny Visser t'Hooft, the remarkable pre-war Karakoram explorer, so he would be on ancestral territory. In addition to Kees, and possibly Robert, we were joined by Julian Freeman Atwood, the appropriately named forester from that part of Shropshire that is for ever Castle Blandings. By late autumn, Fowler had changed his mind.

For the rest of the year Steve and I spent Wednesday nights attempting to cling to the Pump Room ceiling, and recuperating at the pub. The Palmtree was usually crowded. The North London Mountaineering Club met there on Wednesdays. We were always pressed into the corners. One day, just before Christmas, Steve brought over two dripping glasses.

"How's the Ultar application going? Any news from Pakistan?"

"Nazir says the Japanese have failed on it this year. Hasegawa's his name, I think. Unless that's the name of the club."

Steve interrupted me to point at the door. A smart-suited civil servant was pushing his way towards the bar. Mick Fowler. We could hear him shout at the barmaid above the din, "Pint of cheapest bitter . . ."

"Mild's two pence cheaper," shouted back the maid.

"Pint of cheapest mild, please!"

He looked as smug as a cat with two tails as he squeezed over to our corner and turned to me.

"Now then, Victor, are you or are you not climbing with me?"

"I'd be very happy to if . . ."

"Give me your pen and I'll write a contract."

"But don't you think we should see . . ."

"No. Sign this."

The contract was written on the back of a beer mat. It said "I Victor Saunders promise to climb Ultar I with, and only with, Mick Fowler."

I did not realise that in putting my signature to it I had done something I was going to regret. It is not that Mick has a domineering personality, though it is easy to mistake his dislike of discussion for that. He's not a tyrant, just doesn't understand the principle of democracy.

He got the barmaid, giggling and nonplussed, to add her signature to the beer mat, as witness.

"Now back to training for the mountain," he said. "Cheapest mild? Pint?"

"Only problem now is, if I climb with you, Mick, and if Robert can make it, and Steve climbs with him, who is going to climb with Julian?"

"Crags." He had the answer in advance, of course. He went on to explain. "It's all set up. Crags has promised to climb with Julian, and he's rung Julian and it's all fixed up." Mick would never turn up at an award ceremony without the thank you speech in his back pocket. Mr Highly Organised.

We had just six weeks left to take off.

Chapter Nine

You May Go to Your Mountain

The man in the seat in front offered me one of his executive sleeping pills. It was that aficionado of Scottish weekends and chalk Sundays, Duncan Tunstall, on one of his annual pilgrimages to explore the hidden parts of the Karakoram.

"They're really good, Victor. Shell dole them out to all their execs on long journeys. Short-acting sleepers."

"Oh, Duncan, you are such a *yuppie*."

"No, they are really good, you go to sleep for four hours, no hangover, and you arrive feeling rested and ready for action."

Duncan spent the rest of the ten-hour flight banging on about how good the pills were supposed to be. He got pretty excited about it at times.

"You sure they're not amphetamines?"

"*No!* No. Sleepers, I just can't think why they are not working. I was quite sleepy when I took them."

I couldn't sleep either. I was kept awake by the children next to me playing with the light switch, fighting and retching. Duncan leant over to ask them if they'd like to play outside. They looked at him as if he was stupid.

Outside, the view, when it appeared, was Baltic forests. Little Red Riding Hood country. My son, Hugo, would have liked this. We were flying over the land of fairy tales. The last time Britain looked like that it was under the Caledonian Pine.

Across the aisle from me I could guess from the gestures that Julian and Steve were talking about hiring Bazookas for a trial shoot. In Peshawar you can hire any gun from an air pistol to an anti-aircraft cannon, which costs fifty dollars per round. They were clearly going to get through a couple of those. Now they were arguing the size of the bullet hole, Steve holding up one hand with fore-finger and thumb touching, while Julian made a bigger circle of both forefingers and thumbs. In Baltistan the same gesture indicates female. I remember being instructed not to photograph women in Askole. The shepherd raised his thumb to indicate men, and nodded, smiling at the camera, then he made the "female" sign, and shook his head . . . frowning. Sign language. Steve and Julian continued to argue in half sign language about the various merits of the 44 versus the 303. Well, they'd have plenty of time in Peshawar to study the differences.

The view through the porthole turned orange and sandy. Across the desert thin double lines, vehicle tracks, drew endless straight lines, giant curves and incomprehensible small circles. Coming generations of archaeologists might assume they were ley lines, or space messages. Perhaps the lone jeep trail to the nearest Coke machine is really some sort of message after all.

Arriving on the great subcontinent always sets off a deep-seated excitement. For me there is the link to childhood. The heat. I remember Malaya, not with any sort of intellectual comparison; the memory is quite instinctive. The flesh remembers, not the mind. This is how it felt to live in a tropical country. Sweat glands, dormant for years, reawaken. A small part of the brain dictates a slower, more sedate pace to the body.

Half an hour later we were besieged by a frightening band of would-be taxi drivers and porters, each demanding outrageous sums to transport us the five minutes into Rawalpindi cantonment. Our ancient vehicle heeled over at the corners like a yacht, and on the final bend into our hotel, the hub caps flew off across the road, surprising several cyclists and a few pedestrians.

As soon as we had settled in to our grey concrete box labelled Hotel Holiday in red neon, Steve and I arranged to meet Nazir Sabir in the Pearl Continental, a place we could never afford to stay, but the coffee and croissants were good. Nazir Sabir is his country's leading climber and he is also endlessly helpful to visiting Westerners in oiling the wheels and generally pointing us towards our mountains. His smile broadened behind the beard that extended across his face like an unchecked lawn as he listened to our plan.

"We need to stay in Karimabad for about two weeks while we recce and acclimatise, and then we need use of a room as a base while we are on the climb," I explained, rubbing the buttery crumbs down the front of my shirt.

We outlined our need to explore different approaches to the Hidden Pillar, as it did not look too pleasant to descend. Perhaps we would need to examine alternatives. We would want to see the view from the glaciers to the north of Ultar, the Ghulkin or Gulmit Glaciers.

"Yes, yes, some Japanese team was there in 1987."

"Did they find a route?"

"No, they had an avalanche which took away their Camp 1. Then they went round to the Karimabad side."

"Well, we want to try this south-east side. Has anyone ever been on this side?"

"A Polish expedition tried, but could not reach the mountain."

"It's difficult on that side?"

"I think the Hasegawa Route is the easiest. He went from the Karimabad side."

"Up the Ultar nullah?"

"Yes. His Base Camp was the same as yours." He meant our 1984 Bojohaghur expedition. I remembered our Base Camp with warmth. It had apparently become a tourist attraction since then, as it was only a few hours' from the Karakoram Highway.

"So," I summed up, "we will need two or three weeks to acclimatise, and because there is no walk-in, we thought we would spend the time finding a way to this glacier. It's above the village of Mohamedabad on this map."

"Ah yes, the real name is Hametabad. I think there are no hotels there, but you can try Ibrahim Beg in Karimabad. He speaks English."

"Yeah, I know him," Steve volunteered. "He's got a limp arm." Nazir nodded. "I didn't realise so many expeditions have been to Ultar," Steve went on. "It's surprising no one's died on it."

"So far," Nazir replied after a suitably doom-laden pause in which I dripped coffee on my notebook as I tapped the table which I hoped was wooden.

The next few days went by in a hectic rush, interspersed with outbursts from Crags who had packed in the utmost hurry, in between experiments at Imperial College. Crags spent the first morning unpacking his rucksack and having shocked reunions with his gear.

"Oh, eff it, here are my jumars!"

We could hear him from the dining room.

"Christ, my socks!"

"*Oh, eff it!* I can't believe it, all these karabiners, and I accused my cousin . . ."

"Lot of effing there," someone observed.

"Yeah, don't worry, he's fine. That's Effing Crags," said Steve. "His things are made of an alloy new to science, called re-appearium."

Effing Crags came in for breakfast visibly shaken.

In the shaded cool of the Ministry of Tourism, Mr Sidiqui smiled benignly at me as he dictated the last letter for our expedition.

"You have briefed your Liaison Officer?"

I nodded at Captain Amer Ali of the Baluchistan Regiment, and said, "Yes, I am sure we will get on very well." Ali produced one of those extra-special grins that we were to become so used to. All teeth, and big black cow-like eyelashes. Sidiqui turned to Ali.

"And have you examined the equipment the expedition has brought you?"

"Quite satisfactory."

"You may go to your mountain now. Good luck."

Our van for Gilgit was waiting. We had to collect Kees from Islamabad airport on the way, and were also joined for the journey to Hunza by Brian Davidson, who had been to South Georgia with Julian and Kees, where their mountaineering expedition was forced to spend twenty-four consecutive days in a snow hole. Brian was also a scientist, and an unusually bold rock climber.

The van was filled to the brim with our kit. The barrels and tents had been strapped on top. We were squeezed in tighter than in the Palmtree. And there was no beer to anaesthetise the squash. The Karakoram Highway consisted mostly of dry potholes linked by decaying clay-covered tarmac, over which a succession of monstrous giant juke boxes hurtle towards each other.

This was going to be a long journey. I took the opportunity to find out a little more about Crags. I'd been very impressed when I first met the man. We had decided to go rock climbing in North Wales and it poured. Normally the choices are very few in the rain; either the pub, or an easy climb in the wet. Crags had something far more novel in mind. He thought it would be a good idea to climb on Careg Hyldrem near Tremadoc. The route he had in mind was called Primus. I looked it up in the guide book.

"Primus; Brown and Roscoe 1960; 180 feet; E2 4C,5C,4C. Crumbs, that was good for 1960. Hang on a second, we can't climb 5C in the rain, Crags."

"The 5C bit will be dry, Victor."

"Oh, yeah, and what about the top?"

"Oh, that bit's easy."

We finished the climb, hand-jamming a damp crack in the back of the overhanging groove. It was a wonderful position, the rain was so solid that day it was like climbing behind a wall of water. With the last hard lunge, the climb delivered an easy jug over the edge, and into the waterfall. I finished the climb utterly convinced, a believer in Welsh lateral thinking.

The van leapt out of another pothole and I crashed heavily into Crags. Ali was getting excited; we were approaching Abbotabad, Mr Abbot's town, regimental home of the Baluchis. He pointed to ornamental gardens and bungalows with timber columns and verandahs.

After Abbotabad the Highway left the plains and climbed up into acacia jungles, the Himalayan foothills. We had been going five hours, it was dark. We stopped at a roadside tea shop, a string of electric lights hung out over charpoys and rickety tables. The tea was thick with sugar and overboiled milk. Moths and other nightfliers brushed our faces on their way to the light. We sat on the edge of the charpoys, sipping from the tiny cups, listening to the crickets and grasshoppers.

Nine hours out from Rawalpindi we descended to the Indus valley, which we would now follow through increasingly dry country, till we reached the desert leading up to Gilgit. Dawn unveiled the tell-tale signs of a growing tragedy, as we stopped for breakfast at the edge of the great river. From the far bank we noticed a faint and continuous shouting, which was surprising as the river was half a kilometre wide and swollen with the monsoon. Ali said they were wood hunting. Boys were paddling out into the centre of the current on inflated tyres to capture floating timbers. The odd thing was that all the timbers seemed to be the same size. They didn't look at all like flotsam. Further up the Highway the monster juke boxes passed us in convoys, loaded to the gunnels with timber, recognisably the same we had seen floating down stream. Julian, with his forestry hat on, could make neither head nor tail of it. "Perhaps they are cutting down the last Tibetan forest and shipping it into Pakistan; the Chinese are doing that, y'know," he suggested.

By the time we reached Chilas, the desert bandit country south of Gilgit, there were large stacks of the timber lining the road. Neither Steve nor I could remember having ever seen so much timber in the Karakoram. Certainly there was major deforestation going on, but where? Julian said the wood was deodar, a kind of cedar. Somewhere there was an environmental disaster taking place.

It is meant to take fourteen hours to drive from Rawalpindi to Gilgit, but it usually takes twenty-four. Our van heaved and wobbled into the courtyard of the Hunza Inn, and we tumbled out unwashed and vibrating to take a break in Gilgit before finishing off the road journey to Hunza. The Inn was an oasis of cool greenery, with a scattering of white cast iron garden chairs and tables in deep grass. Trellised flowering peas and fruit trees threw dappled shade across the sprawled expedition members.

In the main street a tiny second-hand expedition equipment shop is run by Dad Ali Shah. Dad Ali is a recognisable Hunza man. There are a lot of Hunzakuts in Gilgit, it is only four hours by road from the valley, and Gilgit is the provincial centre. Centuries of isolation have produced not just families, but whole villages with the same broad features, rectangular head and face, hairline straight across the forehead, slightly hooked nose, wide mouth and light-coloured eyes.

Dad Ali looked unflinchingly at us through his pale green eyes.

"Where are you going?"

"Hunza, Ultar. Have you heard any news about the German expedition to Ultar?"

"They have not succeeded, their leader has a broken arm. They were here in Gilgit yesterday, but they have gone to Islamabad."

"What about the Japanese?"

"Hasegawa? He will be here next month. They are going with Nazir Sabir, you know Nazir?" Of course, everyone knew Nazir.

The Japanese team would be large, ten climbers. Their leader, Tsuneo Hasegawa, had made his name soloing the Eigerwand, the Walker Spur and Matterhorn North Face in winter during the late seventies. In 1990 Hasegawa had climbed to within 200 metres of the summit of Ultar. This year he was going to complete his 1990 route on the South-West Face. The Japanese would overlap with us briefly, but it shouldn't be too much of a problem if they were locked into their 1990 route, where all their fixed rope was. We would be snooping around the other side of the mountain. But, choice of route apart, there was still the question of the first ascent. There were no less than three expeditions trying to accomplish this. The mountain had just seen off the Germans. It was now our turn.

Captain Ali met us at Dad Ali's. He had just returned from the District Commissioner's office.

"Do you know about the accident?" he asked me.

"No, what accident?"

"Mr Hillen . . ." he began.

Hillen? Was it the Steve Hillen I knew? And my mind went back to the winter and a phone call from the North. Did I have any pictures of Makrong Kish which was visible from Spantik, but only just? I had put him on to Stephen Venables. In March we had had our Mount Everest Foundation interview for a grant at the Royal Geographical Society. I tried to present myself more or less on time as I remembered that I had once missed an interview completely by falling asleep on the Underground. On that occasion Al Rouse spoke up for our expedition, and later said, leaning on the Clachaig Bar in Glencoe, as I pushed yet another pint at him, "You know, you would have probably got a smaller grant if you had turned up." I am told that was typical of Al. Never a kindness without a dig in the ribs, never a tall story without some grain of home truth.

The screening committee meets in the Council Room of the Royal Geographical Society, with its enormous doors. There is so much oak, it is difficult not to be overwhelmed by the great portals, the panelled walls, the oceanic table. I left the Council Room, wondering if I had convinced the committee that I was fully *compos mentis*, let alone fit to attempt Ultar.

"Hello, Vic." It was the same voice that phoned from the North. "How did it go?" Steve Hillen, in jacket and tie, was looking as uncomfortable as I, as he waited his turn to put the case of the Makrong Kish expedition. "Any advice for the interview?"

"Oh, you'll be all right," I said. It is easy to be blasé after the event. "Just show them that fantastic shot from Kunyang Kish. Let's have a drink afterwards; I'll wait." I waited and we did.

Ali was speaking of two fatalities, of an abseil over a bergschrund from a snow stake which fell out, leaving the leader stranded. He had cramponed down towards the schrund, while his companion climbed up to the same spot. When they should have met, the leader seems to have slipped, falling across the bergschrund and knocking his companion off his feet.

"When did this happen?" I asked.

"Last week, maybe on 10 July. There is only one name so far. The leader was Mr Steve Hillen."

I walked back with Ali, kicking the yellow dust and feeling indescribably sad.

Late that evening our trusty van rolled into Karimabad, in a trail of dust like a Wells Fargo stagecoach.

Chapter Ten

Hunza Days

"Hunza, it means land of the snow. Hun is snow. It is from Tibet, the name they have given to us when they sent their prince to marry our beautiful princess, Bubeli. The prince went back to Tibet to fight wars and Bubeli is still waiting."

Mohamed Shaffar, the timber merchant, pointed up at the spire above Karimabad. "Bublimiting, sometimes it is called Lady's Finger, but this is not so, it is the Throne of Bubeli."

We were standing on the roof of the Mountain Refuge, the vegetarian eating establishment recommended to us by Nazir Sabir. Shaffar and Julian were admiring the circle of mountains above us: Bublimiting, Hunza Peak, Bojohaghur and Ultar, rising 7329 metres above the village, dominated the view to the north.

Six hundred metres below, the wide roaring Hunza river ran its turbulent course towards the Indus, and its long journey through the desert of the Sind. Rising on the far side of the growling brown rapids were the olive-green terraces of the ancient Mirdom of Nagar, Shia country, and the hereditary foes of Ishmaili Hunza. There were stories, which Shaffar would not confirm, though Sustad seemed to know that they were true, that during the long boring winters, the two Mirdoms entertained themselves by taking pot shots at each other across the river.

The fertile oasis that was the Hunza valley stretched ten miles downriver in continuous terraced settlements, but upriver, the lens-shaped bowl of terraced cultivation was closed by huge brown shoulders of moraine and clay, leading up to their respective mountains, Ultar on the Hunza side, and the peaks of the Hispar Glacier on the Nagar side. Our interest was focused on the north side, the true right bank of the river, the flanks of Ultar.

We had come to call the complex of small glaciers under the South East Face, the Hidden Valley. As far as we could make out from our photographs and maps, the entire valley debouched into a narrow gorge above the village the locals called Hametabad and the maps variously Ahmadabad or Mohamedabad. They also located it in different places.

"How long will it take us to walk there?" we asked.

Mohamed Shaffar had the square Hunza face with sad-looking eyes, belied by a wan smile and Hunza cap worn at a cocky angle. He looked like a near-clone of Dad Ali Shah, only his eyes were brown.

"Two hours only . . . it is ten kilometres by the road . . . if you want jeep, I will find my cousin."

The Mountain Refuge was to be our base for the expedition. It consisted of just one poplar-beamed room with wire-netting windows to keep out the flies but let through the cooling wind, a few benches and rough tables spattered with candle wax. A plank served as bookshelf and held a spreading pile of volumes of the kind that passing hippies or trekkers leave behind.

At one end the space was divided by a crude timber serving bar, and beyond that, tending to paraffin burners and cooking, was Hosh Jan, Happy Jan. Jan spoke English and spent several fruitless hours attempting to teach me Burushaski. He worked for the proprietor, Ibrahim Beg, who was known locally as "German". Not "The German", just German. He was meant to be as strong as a stormtrooper. Ibrahim had worked in Bayswater and liked to reminisce late into the night. It was in Bayswater he had been thrown out of a window and lost the use of his right arm.

"So you want a jeep to go to Hametabad, tell me when you want to go, I will get my cousin." Then as an afterthought, massaging his limp right hand:

"Okay, I order you some two-egg armelettes . . . you want tea also?"

It did not matter what you ordered, it always took half an hour. Hosh Jan made good omelettes, fried with onions, tomatoes and chillies, and excellent chips, made from unpeeled Hunza potatoes boiled in ghee.

A Hunza village is a group of houses, often backed onto each other like a human wasps' nest, which derives its water supply from a particular irrigation channel or gotsil. Villages work together on the gotsil they share. The higher the gotsil, the more villages share responsibility for it. Two or three times a year the entire male community will turn out to repair and work on the common canal. In this way the water courses form, not so much a network, but more of a hierarchical stem-and-branch system, with the main trunk located at the glacial torrent, and each village taking for its own one peripheral branch. The channel itself is usually about knee deep and an arm's width across. It may be hacked out of the cliff or, more commonly, based on a ledge with dry-stone walling plugged with sand and grass on the outside edge. Having left the mountain, the water feeds down to the terraced fields, in dripping green lines.

Modern repair and extensions of the system have made extensive use of explosives and machinery, but the control of the water flow is still done by adding or removing weir panels and stones. Some branches have the water switched to them in the morning and other branches in the afternoon. The supply of water is, of course, part of the social structure. In some ways, it *is* the social structure.

We were soon shuffling the narrow dust path beside the Hametabad gotsil. Pebbles rolling off to the right fell a thousand feet into the shadowed gorge below. The sand which we kicked to the left made a plopping, splashing noise in the gotsil's swirling pearly mica. The path to the hill pastures from the village was one of those beautiful short walks that characterise the Hunza valley. It started from the terraced fields where the hydro-culture produces jungles of damp poplar, mulberry, walnut and bamboo. The route was complicated, and we took the precaution of hiring for fifty rupees the services of a shepherd, Taighrun Shah, to lead us through to the edge of the glacier we had glimpsed from the road. It was cool because we started out at dawn. Another sensible precaution. The hot part of the day was not for walking around in. A short climb by a tumbling waterfall, overhung with creeping plants, led by ancient stone steps, to the main channel, warming in the weak glare of the early-morning sun.

This valley had been Islamic for centuries, yet the shrine at the start of the canal looked like a pre-Buddhist shrine of place. On a pinnacle above the canal, just where it started to cut into the cliff, a crown of stones, with prayer flags and horns, spoke of a time when the men and women of Hunza held beliefs more ancient and magical than either Islam or even Buddhism. The shrine might have been some kind of a relic of Bon Po, the shamanistic religion which was absorbed by Buddhism in the same way that the pagan solstice rites were absorbed into Christian Easter.

Shrines such as these occur across the Himalaya on the fringes of
Tibetan culture, often at the last safe resting place before a dangerous
passage. We too could sense the awe and danger walking along the
gotsil, with its huge precipice on one side and gently overhanging
wall on the other. I guessed the people of Hametabad had stopped
to pray here for generations, but my command of sign language was
quite insufficient for the task of quizzing Taighrun about this.

The path on the rampart swung out on to the cliff, and into the
shadow of the Hametabad gorge. It was perfectly level and for
almost a kilometre led across the blank rockface. On the opposite
side of the gorge, blank granite walls over 300 metres high also
had a thin green line drawn across the centre with no apparent
means of support. Another gotsil. You do not walk *in* the gotsil,
of course. The path is on its outer rampart, with no balustrade, and
the changing perspective of the gorge bottom rushing past your feet
can be disorientating. So you trail the fingers of one hand against the
rock where possible, until, thankfully, the valley floor rises up to meet
the channel.

The tiny rampart led to the edge of a wide torrent. A few minutes
of scrambling behind Taighrun brought us over a rickety wire and
wood bridge on to a steep moraine. A glacial draught swept down the
bed of the gorge, making the crossing of the small bridge memorable
for the noise, the windiness and the first sensation of cold of the
expedition.

"That's katabatic!" said Crags. "It's Scottish, by God!" said
Julian in his safari shorts. Taighrun followed the crest of a residual
moraine. Half an hour's steep walking through the yellow gorse and
willow scrub brought us onto the terraces of an abandoned village
called Gourpie. This was the lowest of the summer pastures above
Hametabad. Around the broken huts were scattered clusters of
desert rose, the *sia*, from which the Siachen Glacier derives its name.
Searing walls of burnt orange granite reaching high closed the view.
The watercourse traced a line of dark green, a ribbon of willow and
poplar thickets across the ochre browns of the desert scrub.

Above Gourpie the canyon opened just enough to show a sliver of
a high black tower, and a silver cornice. Crags pointed it out to Julian.
Julian said, "By George!" We all stared. A tremble of excitement ran
through the party as we realised that we had seen the Hidden Pillar
for the first time.

Taighrun left us as we argued about the best place to erect our
tents. There were goat and sheep droppings in the remains of the

huts, some of which still had their roofs and were clearly still being used as sheep pens.

Crags and Julian pitched their Quasar on a flat patch at the entrance of a hut. Steve and Brian put their tent a little further from the main sheep tracks, and Kees and I found that the only flat spot to attract us was the roof of a hut.

"You'll get flea-bitten," warned Steve.

"I am counting on the roof having been smoked by countless generations of shepherds," I replied.

"Then you'll get cancer," said Steve. "And you'll break the roof." He had a point, it was creaking. But in the morning Kees and I had escaped the flea bites, while the others looked like they had just acquired the measles.

We were just cooking our supper when out of the hills a small flock of sheep and goats overran our position, under the lax control of a spotty youth who introduced himself to us in English.

"My name is Mohamed Isar." He had with him not only fifty animals but also half a dozen small children. "I come from Hametabad. This place is called Gourpie. Can I help you?" We offered him a neighbourly cup of tea, but he produced his own brew, a large handful of thyme. "We call it *tomorro chai*."

His tea was indeed very good.

"Shepherds drink this," he said.

"Do you drink it to help with the altitude, for going higher?" I asked.

"No. We can pick it on the mountain. It is growing everywhere." The simple explanation. He spoke English with some fluency, so we asked about the shrine with the flags.

"Some people, they pray for a son, or maybe something good. But it is not certain, because it is not Islamic . . . The old gods are not so strong."

Presumably the old gods were on their way to becoming mere superstition. But the children seemed to be the true keepers of folklore. When asked about a kind of ghost called the *parih*, Mohamed Isar turned to the twelve-year-olds, who told us that *parihs* were in fact yetis with wings, whose feet pointed backwards, and that they have not been seen since the time of the forefathers. The children knew this, yet the adults had forgotten. I was reminded of J.M. Barrie's *Peter Pan*, where grown-ups knew nothing of Never Never Land. Crags said that backward-pointing feet is a standard feature of bogeymen across the globe.

Mohamed Isar and his small army of children and sheep trickled downhill, but not before he had left us with a crude map, a sort of geographical naming of the parts. The ravine we found ourselves in was the Hametabad nullah, flowing from the snout of the Hametabad Glacier, at about the same level as Gourpie. Above Gourpie the nullah narrowed into a canyon, and the cramped pastures of Sina and Kunus. The goat track to Sina climbed convex slabs for 300 metres above Gourpie. Above Sina, we could see there was an icefall, which poured out of the hidden valley, where it was fed by the seven separate glaciers. The next day we would begin our explorations in earnest.

We would visit Sina and find a route to the Hidden Valley. Joy. Excitement.

The evening sun caught the orange tips of the granite spires above us. With pint brews of *tomorro* warming our hands, the evening passed as Brian told us of his recent experience to Broad Peak. He was supposed to be guiding a commercial expedition, but had suffered a retinal haemorrhage half-way up the mountain. I asked if he thought it was really possible to "guide" an 8000-metre mountain, but he was not to be drawn.

The next day was 18 July. The sky was clear. Beads of sweat glistened on Steve's neck ahead of me, the back of his tee shirt was damp. There was a faint perfume of turpentine from the stunted pine and dwarf juniper. Steve turned round. Behind him was Ultar framed by the canyon walls. The mountain was magnificent, even more compelling than the photographs. Between the walls, the ice of the seven glaciers of the Hidden Valley spilled in a frozen jumble for 300 metres or more. We examined the icefall closely.

Sometimes it *is* possible to pick a relatively safe route through steep icefalls. The Khumbu Icefall on Everest, the Uzbenski Icefall on Ushba, and others rely on the climber getting through the danger zone in an acceptably short time. But not here. The Sina Icefall looked too steep and long for safe passage. The ice-smoothed red walls either side held no ramps, ledges or gullies that might lead from the lower glacier to the upper. It was true that the right side of the icefall looked a little less steep than the left side, but as we watched there sprouted little brown blossoms on the left side of the barrier, followed at a few seconds by the distant report, as of gunfire. Rockfall. I didn't think this boded particularly well for either side. Steve shook his head.

"No, Victor."

"No? I suppose we'd better tell Crags and Julian."

I felt depressed.

Chapter Eleven

Into the Hidden Valley

The next day the sun shone. It shone every single day in Karimabad, no matter how foul the weather on Ultar, and it often was utterly foul. I think the way the mountain stands alone at the end of the Batura chain seems to attract storms. Yet it remains dry in the villages. Sometimes you can see the clouds from Ultar forming rain over the Hunza river in a dark grey wash which rarely reaches the ground. The drops just evaporate on their way down.

Crags spent the morning washing his clothes, which brought admiration from Captain Ali, our Liaison Officer. Crags explained.

"It comes from working on board ship. Everyone, even the Captain, washes their own." Captain Ali was so impressed that he took up clothes washing from that day. Not so Julian, who simply collared the nearest likely-looking native and handed over his bundle of clothes. Steve and I didn't seem to need washing of any kind. Steve went further, and made a pact with Ali not to shave till the end of the trip. Already the two of them were ragged faced.

Having disposed of his laundry, Julian found Mohamed Shaffar at the local sawmill and asked him about the timber we had seen on the road. In favourable conditions deodars grow to a height of 70–80 metres, taking perhaps 100 years to reach that size. Shaffar said that the timber was being felled from hills high above Besham and Chilas on the Highway and, no, he did not think the forest was being replaced. Later Julian discovered that the police would not guarantee safe passage to inspect the logging. It all looked very sad. The presence of the new efficient Karakoram Highway made transport easy, so deforestation was proceeding without any apparent control.

Shaffar was also the local historian and, after telling us about the timber, he mentioned he had a film of D.L. Lorimer, dating from 1935. Incredible! Lorimer on film! The last Englishman to speak the Hunza language, Burushaski, fluently was one of my enthusiasms and it was extremely difficult to track down fresh information about him. We were promised a film show after tea.

The reality of the film was stranger than I had expected.

"What on earth's that?"

"That is the *bitten*. Women prophets," said Shaffar. "There are no real *bitten* any more. Now they are men and they dance for the tourists."

The *bitten*, caught for all time in jerky black and white, were whirling ecstatic female oracles. The sight was strongly reminiscent of the Oracle of Shey, a fragment of shamanism which had been adopted by the Buddhism of Ladakh. Suddenly, I knew we had been right to look at the Hametabad shrine as a religious fossil. The realisation fed and filled my imagination. It was meant to be a mountaineering expedition, but this is why I returned to the Himalaya. Discovery is not always about physical boundaries, nor even about finding things no one has known before. Discovery can be quite personal, putting things together in a way that suddenly makes sense. I love it. Discovery is the meaning of life.

It was dark, the path back to our rooms wound through waist-high weeds and apricot groves. The headtorches pick out the way like searchlights. Lorimer's silent film was still running in my mind. There used to be wine-making, and though the wheat is still hand-reaped, a Massey Ferguson is now used to drive a threshing unit in Hunza, though outlying villages still have the threshing circle and tethered ox that Lorimer saw. Perhaps the most arresting difference was today's ubiquitous jeep, where only horses were used fifty years ago. Whole families travelled on a single pony in the film, which provoked Sustad to remark that the last place he'd seen anything like it was Morocco, but there the locals took pleasure in cruelty to their animals.

"So what're you two doing tomorrow?" Crags asked.

"What about the side valley next to Gourpie?" suggested Steve.

"Yes, OK," I agreed. "Mohamed Isar must have seen more than is visible from Sina in order to know about the seven glaciers. So there must be another way into the upper valley."

Julian and Crags were not interested; they would prefer to examine the Japanese route above Karimabad.

"At least we know we can reach the mountain that way, old chap."

For the next week the team split into separate search parties, Crags and Julian looking at the Hasegawa line which they had identified through the binoculars as a sort of huge Tower Ridge, while Steve and I continued with our attempts to reach the Hidden Valley from Hametabad.

We spent three days based at the shepherds' camp of Barabares, struggling to cross 4000-metre cols that we hoped would give us a clear view of the seven-fingered glacier, and gave up in disquiet. The cols led to horrible abysses and unattainable pinnacles, which we tried turning on both left and right. It was our first visit to the snowline, and as I gasped for breath in the thin air I made the serious mistake of saying I felt a little "altitudish", which provoked a lecture on English usage from Steve,

"I've noticed that 'ish' is really common in England, but is only used by high school students at home. It's typical bad English. No wonder the editor of the Oxford English Dictionary says the centre of the English language is now in the United States."

"Rubb-ish!" I said with I hoped argument-disposing emphasis.

Then for three days we visited the cols that we hoped would overlook the Hidden Valley. We gave up in despair. "Never seen anything like it. It must be the hardest valley to get into in the world."

I had a horrible vision: of spending the entire expedition failing to reach even the bottom of the route.

Back at Hametabad, Mohamed Isar introduced us to Gulam Rasul who told us we had been barking up the wrong *haguts*. *Haguts*, I now realised, was the Hunza word for col. Across the valley, in the Nagar dialect of Burushaski, the word is *duasum*. I had already spent several frustrating hours trying to pronounce *duasum* in different ways, to the amused curiosity of passing shepherds.

Having pointed out that we had been to the wrong pass, Gulam offered – for a high price – to show us the way taken by the only person to have reached the Hidden Valley, a long-dead hunter. I wondered if even Edward Whymper had ever been as dubious about the claims of his shepherd guides as we were of ours.

The next day, during the 2500-metre climb back to Barabares with Gulam, we sat out the heat of the noon sun at the abandoned hamlet of Gourpie, resting in the shade of a willow tree, our feet in the brook, our backs against a rock. The light formed dappled shadows and small leaves of silver, flickering over the earth, stones and our bare legs. The stream made a sound that was itself dappled. "A googol," said Steve, "is ten to the power of one hundred, but a googolplex is a googol to the power of a googol." We spent half an hour trying to work out how many noughts there should be after the one. Steve eventually came to the obvious conclusion: "There are so many noughts, we cannot comprehend it." Our brains too had become dappled.

In the evening we reached Barabares, a shepherd's hut with a large covered sheep and goat pen attached. Barabares, at about 4000 metres, was the one camp that Hametabad seemed to maintain all summer. There were 200 sheep and goats in the lush high pastures. We pitched our Supernova, and after a supper of pickled herrings and biscuits Gulam invited us to join him in the single smoke-blackened room, on the sleeping area, divided from the main earth floor by a poplar beam. The shepherd prodded the fire, and lit a K2 cigarette with an ember. The pot boiled, and he passed us a pair of unsavoury enamel mugs containing salt tea. I have never liked salt tea, and this was particularly foul. Drinking it was a race between finishing the brew and retching.

In the morning we left Barabares with Gulam, the tidal wave of sheep and goats surging from their corral and all round our legs. Three hours later we stood at a col that Steve and I had previously dismissed. Gulam pointed across the most repulsive collection of ravines to a distant gap in a pinnacled ridge.

I had understood that Kai Kunuso was the name of the Hidden Valley, but now I was not so sure. It seemed more likely to mean something like, "where only the seriously demented might want to go". The sides of the ravines consisted of precariously balanced boulders over an apparently bottomless abyss. Three more cols followed in succession, separated by increasingly frightening ravines, each echoing with rockfalls that our tired feet dislodged.

At the third col we caught sight of the Great Barrier Icefall. Compared with these ravines it looked a doddle. "Hey Steve, it looks all right down there after all," I shouted above the din of rolling boulders and collapsing mountainside.

Steve turned to look just as a section of hillside the size of an office building decided to break away and sweep our proposed line through the icefall. "Looks like someone is trying to tell us something," he murmured.

On the fourth col Steve let out a blood-curdling howl. Wheezing and puffing like an overheated jalopy, I found Gulam sitting serenely by the wildly gesticulating American.

"This is it. He has done it. Look, there is the glacier. This is Kai Kunuso!" But Gulam was looking at the sand by his feet, where the paw prints of a snow leopard showed that our valley, beyond the Pass of the Shifting Stones, was far from uninhabited.

This time the long run down to Hametabad was a joyous and exciting affair. As usual, our jeep driver was waiting. His name was Fidel Hussein of the Magnificent Moustache. Wherever we went, from Karimabad to Hametabad, from Hametabad, up to Gulkin, or down to Aliabad in search of the hot springs, Fidel's jeep always seemed to be waiting for us, which was odd, because he denied being the cousin of Ibrahim, or of Shaffar, or anyone else who had promised to fix us up with transport. Although he had a pleasant manner, and rarely overcharged us, Fidel had the horrid habit of missing gears on the corners, and occasionally missing the brake pedal too. The steeper the drop beyond the corner, the more certain he was to miss his pedal. So it was not just the thought of armelettes that made us grateful to arrive at the refuge after each journey.

We got back to find half the North London Mountaineering Club had arrived with the newly wed Mick. His father, George, and Crags' better half, Sue, our old friend Sonja Vietoris and her Bengali companion Hasina were all at the Mountain Refuge. Crags and Sue booked a room in a hotel miles from us – at our insistence. We didn't want to be kept awake.

Mick lost no time in berating me. "Exactly who is climbing with whom?" and "Stop dithering, man!" and "Are you or are you not climbing with me?" "Well, I think we should see," I said, bringing on yet another exasperated inquisition.

Steve, who was devouring his four-egg chilli armelette and a huge bowl of chips, cleared his mouth just long enough to say, "Go with the flow, Mick. We've all been on enough expeditions to know that things change daily – it always sorts itself out – "

By now Mick was having apoplectic fits. "Go with the flow" does not translate into Fowler's English. Steve just grinned and began to pour a gallon of *tomorro chai* down his throat. I sipped at my chipped cup; it was delicious, thyme flavoured with cardomom pods.

But there was a solution staring us in the face; Julian was not, in any case, interested in the Hidden Pillar. He recognised that 4000 metres of difficult climbing was beyond his experience. (It was beyond all of our experiences.) And now he was having doubts even about the Hasegawa Route. This left Crags free to team up with Mick, while Julian helped Kees with the filming. So Crags and Mick set off for a training jaunt up the Hassanabad Glacier which fills the valley system to the north-west, and Steve and I decided to do our acclimatising on the same ridge, approached from the Ultar Gorge. We were going to follow a route we had taken six years earlier on Ultar's neighbour, Bojohaghur, to about 6000 metres.

We bivouacked on a ledge 1000 metres up an immense snow slope, after climbing a series of dry avalanche runnels during the night, and sat out the dangerous daylight hours. Before setting off I felt morbid and sent down my notebooks with Kees, with instructions to forward them to Maggie in the last resort.

As if on cue, at 7.00 a.m., when the sun first began to light up the face above us, a boulder the shape and size of a car wheel was released by the sun, and began to slither down the ice and snow, till it gathered enough momentum to tumble, then roll, accelerating straight towards our bivouac for 100 metres till it struck a small outcrop and bounced clear of our imprisoning sleeping bags. We could not have moved out of its way had we tried. The heat then turned all the avalanche runnels on like taps. Great outpourings of wet slurry mixed with gravel and rocks and chunks of ice roared down the chutes beside us. We ate breakfast shouting to be heard above the din. "Some whisky?" bellowed Steve, and half filled my cup with a poisonous Chinese distillation which had probably been dyed yellow, though Ibrahim insisted it was good stuff. I raised the cup to my lips when Steve pointed at the sky. Clay pigeons! Dozens of them! All coming our way! Steve pulled his sleeping bag over his head. I dived for the shelter of a small ledge, hoping not to miss, as there was nothing below for at least 1000 metres. When the bombardment was over I climbed back to find Steve still sipping his whisky. He told me a story about W.C. Fields, who had been not only a comic actor but also a master juggler and stunt man who could tumble down stairs without spilling his Martini. I looked at my cup. The contents had been completely replaced with wet snow. This was the last straw.

"What I really want to do is technically difficult routes which are absolutely safe," said Steve. "But alarm bells are going off, and it's not just this rockfall. I am getting nervous. The climbing I am really enjoying, but when I am not climbing I am worrying. Perhaps we are just getting too old for this. How you feeling about it?"

"I don't remember being this worried," I agreed. "It is possible, I suppose, that we are just frightening each other."

"I slept rather badly."

"So did I. I had a dream. We were in a great arena. Before us sat an Indian chief. On one side of him were young chiefs and a Japanese climber. On the other side were his family. They were American Indians, but were also Burushaski. This is the logic of dreams. The chief spoke at length in a thickly accented and broken English, laced with a stream of Burushaski. Then he turned to us. Why climb Ultar, and why climb our route rather than the much easier Hasegawa route?

"We explained about the Hidden Valley and the Hametabad Glacier, and why it was so exciting to find new and unvisited corners; the Japanese climber interrupted to say that no such valley existed. 'Yes, it does,' we said. 'But you can only see it for two minutes as you drive up the KKH.' The young chiefs agreed volubly with us and the Japanese climber disappeared. Then we explained why we wanted to climb the Hidden Pillar. We spoke of its size, almost 4000 metres. And as we talked I noticed that one by one the family and young chiefs were disappearing. We talked of the compulsion of the pillar and the safe route by which we would try to climb it. The more we talked the fewer remained to hear us. The great chief disappeared, and when tea was brought, we saw that we were now alone."

"And what does all that mean?" asked Steve.

"I don't know, maybe the chief and his family represent our doubts about the route, which disappear as we build a proper plan."

"I think it means you're just too boring for people to stay and listen," said Steve kindly. "I think we'd better go down tonight, just as soon as it gets cold." He rolled another cigarette. He had been chewing Nicorettes all day. So much for giving up fags, the gum had merely increased his need for the nicotine. Now he was chewing gum, and dragging on a cigarette simultaneously. "Are you frightened? (chew, drag) This is literally the first time I have felt apprehension about a route (drag, puff, chew), ever. In fact, Victor (chew, chew), if you said you were frightened too, and wanted to go rock climbing (drag, puff), I'd join you for the next four weeks (chew, chew, chew)." It's like conversing with an asthmatic cow, I thought to myself. We abseiled out that night, reaching the Mountain Refuge for supper the next evening.

The candles were guttering in the breeze that swept through the Mountain Refuge. This was candle night. Alternate nights there was electricity. Dusty and tired, we had ordered plates of Hosh Jan's wonderful chips and four-egg omelettes: Steve asked for extra chillies to go with his blanket of tomato ketchup. Sitting next to Steve was Gulam Karim Mukarim, of the Karakoram Writers Forum. A poet of Burushaski religious love. He was reading the *Nicomachean Ethics* in the Refuge. Steve was intrigued. "Where else in the Himalaya do you find locals reading Aristotle?"

"Not so surprising," said Gulam Karim. "You think the Greeks are at the heart of your culture, but you forget they are also the heart of ours." Then he put a question to us: "The Koran asks: is he who goes groping on his face more rightly guided – or he that walks upright on a beaten road?"

"Just about sums up expeditions," said Steve. "To fail on new routes or walk up the boring old ones."

There was a travelling hippie at the next bench, black bearded, brown skinned, soft leather waistcoat and bare arms with bracelets. Two Hunzakuts and Ibrahim sat with him, entranced. The traveller showed them his palms, then turned his hands palm down. He rolled his fingers into a pair of tight fists. The audience nodded. The man swiftly rotated and opened his fists, and a silent explosion of red silk scarfs leapt in the air. Ibrahim smiled his crooked smile, his friends laughed and clapped and asked the magician to do it again. It was a world away from the fear and fright of avalanches and rockfall.

In another corner, two young Hunzakuts, in Hunza hats and Shalwar suits, were playing with a cretin dressed in rags. There are lots of those in the iodine-deficient Karakoram. The lads shook their shoulders, and the grinning cretin shook his body, then the lads tapped their elbows and the boy slapped his arms. Then the lads tapped their cheeks, making the cretin slap his own face.

It had been a long day. Tomorrow Steve and I were going back to Hametabad, and after that would carry loads up to the Hidden Valley, maybe even try to climb the mountain. I staggered off to read Primo Levi's *Periodic Table*. One of Levi's ancestors was Barbasachin, Sachin equals Isaac. Here, in Burushaski, an analogous transposition occurs in a word (one of many) for thank you. Ishkuria, derived from the Urdu *chukuria*. I had got to the chapter called Steel, about Sandro Delmaestro, and mused about the names Sandro, Sasha and Sikander, all derived from Alexander, as is my name. Delmaestro was murdered by a fifteen-year-old fascist.

I fell asleep with the book in my hand and dreamt. It was another odd dream, all mixed bits from the last few days, full of anxiety.

There was a land where people beat their donkeys mercilessly, and this land was called Morocco. People would stand and stare while a boy murderer, carrying a machine-gun, beat tied-up donkeys for no apparent reason. Friends gathered in the apricot grove with greetings such as *Gruss Gott*, which is the same as *Allah al Akhbar*, to stand in the shade and watch the boy beat the living daylights out of the imprisoned ass who, being tethered by his hindleg, could no more escape the beating than the mountain sheep can escape the rain. The large eyes and immense ears sought no help from the amused onlookers passing the time of day, showed no self-pity, only an anxiety to avoid the next blow. But this donkey was different. It was enchanted. It was a dreaming donkey, and if you could see under those large eyelashes (like the ones my mother had to use in the sixties) to see into those large liquid eyes and beyond into the very thoughts of the animal, you would see the intelligent creature's mind at work.

A crowd of donkeys gathered in the shade to watch a juvenile Moroccan, tethered by his ankle. An ancient donkey approached the boy, but being of a tender cast of mind, did not beat the Moroccan, but instead lifted a foreleg. The Moroccan lifted his arm in imitation. The crowd of donkeys hee-hawed. The ancient one shivered his haunches and the boy shook his shoulders. The crowd brayed their appreciation. The old ass bucked, and the boy jumped. The old one pawed his hind quarters, and the young one slapped his thighs. The donkey (with an effort of contortion extraordinary for such an old animal) landed his hoofs on his back, and the boy struck himself on his own back. The crowd heed and hawed and the old one nodded, and with each nod the young delinquent beat himself till he fell senseless to the ground.

The large eyelashes flickered and the liquid black eyes lazily followed the movement of the next blow from the fifteen-year-old, who was still carrying his submachine-gun across his shoulders.

The villagers, gathered in the apricot shade, watched listlessly under the noon day sun while the boy thrashed the animal, which had stopped running away, and stood and stared at the boy, watching the next blow fall. The donkey lifted his foreleg, and the boy, mesmerised by the act, as a rabbit is mesmerised by the wagging tail of a creeping fox, raised his hand. The donkey brought down his hoof and the boy brought down his gun. With an effort of contortion extraordinary for such an old animal, the ass brought down his hoofs together in such a way that the Moroccan, imitating him, pointed the gun at his own head and depressed the trigger. The crowd, agape and gasping under the trees, watched as the Moroccan boy shot himself with a burst of machine-gun fire, showering the heavens with lead and pelting the crowd with blood.

The Magnificent Moustache drove Steve, Kees, Julian and me to Hametabad the next day. The first person we met on stepping out of our dust-mobile was Mohamed Isar who agreed to collect a few porters for us, leaving us free to wander round Hametabad till the next day. For thirty rupees the village lunatic showed us the way to the hydro-electric plant which makes this village rather special. A 300-metre drop via a 30 cm steel pipe and a huge tap-wheel provided the power for a simple turbine which in turn drove a small generator and was controlled by a domestic fuse board. We were told by Mohamed Isar that the plant delivered 500 kilowatts. The whole set-up was housed in a traditional stone-walled and poplar-beamed house. The lunatic led us up to the top of the pipe where we could see the water came from the usual gotsil with wooden slats to control the flow, which was off during the day.

The village elder called Ali Mahdad invited us to wait for Mohamed Isar in his orchard, which had goat-cropped grass, a pearly stream and five or six apricot trees, enclosed by a dry-stone wall. Unlike Shiites, Ishmaili women will greet you in the street, even in the northern areas, but they are still a tad short of liberation. Ali called for his wife and instructed her to prepare tea for us. Next he brought out a four-metre rod to beat the trees and produce a rain of ripe apricots which rolled down the slope chased by his grandchildren. Some of them were enormous, the size of peaches, but the best were those green-just-turning-ripe. They had a flavour at once both sour and flowery. I could think of no better taste. What a terrible pity that I am allergic to apricots. After the first half-dozen my mouth had begun to sting and burn as if I had been eating raw nettles.

I was interested to see Ali's house and he showed us round. The main room, the *har*, was square, with four columns which defined a central seating area, two sleeping platforms and an entrance well; overhead, a square hole in the ceiling lets out air and smoke and is formed by a series of diagonal pendentives. This was the feature that surprised me. I had only expected it in the grander houses. In one corner of the room was the ubiquitous tin trunk – the only form of storage space. From the outside the buildings look like Mexican pueblos – stone walls plastered with mud, poplar beams and twig-matting roofs, likewise mud plastered, with trays of apricots drying on them. Electric light in the living room and kitchen was supplied nightly by the hydro-power plant and controlled by crude switch and fuse boards.

Ali Mahdad said his apricots went to Lahore, Karachi and England. He showed off his 12-bore and Chinese 303 (bolt action, five rounds in the mag plus one up the spout), Kees showed him his Aaton. Ali told Julian about the chakor, ram chakor, nilgai, markor and other creatures he had shot at with the guns. Meanwhile Kees was telling Ali Mahdad one of his rare jokes, about when he was introduced to Justin. "Kees this is Justin . . . Justin – Kees." This did not translate very well into Burushaski.

After tea Ali Mahdad took us on an architectural tour of the village, the high point being a visit to a nearly finished house built by a deaf mute, Shezat Ali. Shezat was a master carpenter, and the house plan was similar to Ali Mahdad's, which reinforces the impression that vernacular architecture is alive and well in Hunza. The carving of the columns was particularly ornate. Steve and Shezat exchanged professional pleasantries about carpentry joints, and drew each other crafty diagrams. Not to be outdone, I drew them a traditional Japanese joint. Shezat, deaf mute though he was, became very excited, indicating good and bad points of our joints, and drew what he indicated was a local joint. That evening Steve said this had been the best day of the trip.

We slept in the *har* of a village elder with only one thumb. There were plates and plates of chicken curry, dhal of various kinds, aloo, fresh tomatoes, spring onions and chilli and chapatis. We gorged ourselves. One Thumb's food was the best we had had to date. We sprawled out and talked to One Thumb about the buildings, how the design proceeded from generation to generation with minor improvements by succeeding artisans. The houses throughout the Hunza valley were variations on a single theme, but even more striking perhaps was the *yengutz*, the flour mill. The design is standard across the Himalayan chain from the Hindu Kush to Bhutan and so suggests Tibetan influence. We were all very taken with the Himalayan flour mill, but could not understand one modification we saw here, where the entire timber turbine was lifted by wire to control the power. It seemed so much easier to block the flow of water. Presumably this is a modification that will not survive into future generations. Probably not all the mills will. Villages on the edge of the Karakoram Highway now use diesel to grind their wheat.

We were woken by the sound of singing. It was the Hametabad village school at assembly. We rushed out to see the children in their neat little uniforms. The school building was another vernacular flat-roofed house, by the *gama khana*, the mosque. Above the village were dark shadows crossing the ravines, gotsils dripping water and trailing vegetation like hanging gardens. Walking up to Gourpie we found Gulam and Mohamed Isar engaged with dozens of others removing boulders from the canal. Sustad remarked that "half the village must be here." "Yes," said Kees, "the male half." We recognised almost every man we had met so far, Isar, Gulam, Shezat, the grinning old shepherds and One Thumb. One Thumb explained the community was cleaning the gotsil, which happened every three months.

Chapter Twelve

First Ascent of Hunza Peak

Meanwhile Mick and Crags were exercising themselves on the Hasanabad Glacier. In Mick's words, "I had assumed our proposed route would only require one rope and hardly any gear. Crags contributed by forgetting his helmet." Fortunately, some hospitable Swedes lent them rope, gear, helmet and dehydrated food. As a bonus they learnt that their benefactors had just climbed Bublimiting (5850m) and left all the necessary abseil points in place. Mick and Crags decided to climb the col at 5600 metres between Bublimiting and Hunza Peak and "take it from there". Here is Mick's account of what followed.

Bublimiting is one of those peaks that is talked about and pointed at an awful lot but appears to get very few ascents. The main reason for the lack of success seems to be that parties historically tend to attempt the climb from Ultar nullah, where the French team of Patrick Cordier and Jacques Martin made the first ascent in 1982. This involved an ascent up the repugnant south-east side of the col between Bublimiting and Hunza Peak which has, to the best of my knowledge, repulsed all other would-be second ascensionists. From the north-west, or Hassanabad side, though, a straightforward ice slope, steepening to 55 degrees, leads directly to the col. Facing north-west it also stays out of the sun till 10.30 a.m., a real bonus at these altitudes. We climbed this slope in two days with an interim bivouac on a ledge at 4700 metres. Unfortunately, so much effort was put into constructing this ledge that the back wall became rather unstable and collapsed onto the tent, breaking one of the poles, luckily without injuring the occupants.

The next day a 900-metre pull up one of those interminable 50-degree ice slopes thoroughly exercised the lungs and finally led to the elusive col which proved to be of hard ice, seriously corniced and generally very unfriendly in terms of bivouac positions. A promising hanging balcony beneath the cornice failed to survive my jumping up and down to test its strength and at length we settled for hacking a precarious ledge out of the cornice and securing ourselves against collapse with ice screws well back from the edge.

Bublimiting looked surprisingly close and in fact only four rope-lengths took us to the summit the next morning. Even more surprising was the fact that the easiest route up this stunning rock pinnacle (when seen from the Ultar nullah side) is actually almost all snow and ice with a hidden arête providing reasonable 50-degree ice climbing to the final six-metre rock pinnacle.

Flushed with the success of Bublimiting and back on the still precarious tent platform (increasing familiarity failed to make it feel any more secure), there seemed little excuse for not taking advantage of the perfect weather and "taking a look" at the West Ridge of the unclimbed Hunza Peak (6250m) on the other side of the col.

This ridge is in fact more of a face to begin with until, at about 6050 metres, it develops into a snow ridge with huge cornices overhanging the Ultar side.

It was clearly further than Bublimiting and in recognition of this we made the decision to leave the tent on the col but to take sleeping bags in case of any unexpected nights out. Our concern was to prove to be well founded.

After somehow taking two and a half hours to get organised, a 5.30 a.m. start saw us grappling with the first difficulties at daybreak under a cloudless sky. Excellent quality granite with snow-choked fault lines was the order of the day and, with only intermittent difficulties, progress was relatively fast. Crags led a difficult slanting rock gangway and I led a thin ice streak through steep walls before altitude took its weary toll and the pace slowed to a crawl on 50–55-degree ice slopes plastered in powder and baked by temperatures known only to the Karakoram sun. Monstrous cornices overhung the Ultar nullah side with an obviously exhausting snow ridge ahead. We abandoned our rucksacks for the final stage to the summit. Snow varying from soft to horrific led the way forward and at 4.00 p.m. we stood on our first unclimbed Himalayan summit. Too tired for real celebrations, we took summit photos of each other and collapsed to admire the superb views. It was fourteen days since I had left London.

Having descended to Karimabad, via an uncomfortable night when we failed to get back to the tent and my contact lens fluid froze solid, I must admit the temptation to rush back to England whilst the going was good was great indeed. After all, I could be back at my civil service desk, not to mention my wife, with two peaks, one of them previously unclimbed, under my belt, having only taken three weeks of my annual leave entitlement. However, Ultar was our main objective, and further exertion was inevitable.

Chapter Thirteen

What Goes Up

Mists rolled into the Hidden Valley. In the centre of the valley, at the junction of the seven glaciers, an island of pinnacles rose above the fog like frozen music. Later it caught a burst of sunshine, grey mists threaded Tibetan scarves through the spires. Julian said: "This is as beautiful as South Georgia, that's how beautiful it is." Kees and Julian had helped us carry our loads into the valley. After lunch they would leave us, and return to Hametabad. There was a distant roar of séracs and couloirs avalanching.

We had two kinds of instant mash, Sainsbury's and Yeomans, but having disposed of the wrappers didn't know which was which and this was a pity as one kind was delicious, the other inedible. Life is a lottery, we did not know which packets to take up the hill. The conversation turned to food.

Steve	I like nothing better than two or three pasties in the Star, with a couple of pints, having just done a new route on the shale.
Kees	I prefer the Stilton which you have to scoop out with a spoon.
Steve	Doug brought one of those to Makalu, it got soft enough to eat just as we were about to leave Base Camp.
Kees	With port.
Steve	But I prefer a good Logger.
Kees	Logger?
Victor	He means lager, Kees.
Julian	Are you sure?

Whooooosh . . . whooooosh . . . two black shapes making a noise like a turbo jet shot past the tents. Julian said they were ram chakor, snow cocks, and damn good sport too. They fly so fast they're really hard to hit.

After lunch Kees and Julian left us alone with the wildlife. As we had crossed the pass earlier an ibex and her fawn had watched us for fifteen minutes from the top of a boulder. Later four of the elusive creatures scrambled to escape us by climbing pinnacles I would not dream of setting foot on without a rope. Down by the glacier were two sets of large cat tracks, though we never saw any other sign of the snow leopard that Gulam said lived here. Also, by the spring from which we drew our water, were signs of marmot. Lamagai, ram chakor and birds of various sizes and colours also inhabited the valley. We were not really alone at all.

We spent our first night in the valley climbing the start of the Hidden Pillar. There was a steep gully that led up through the first tower. This was a daytime avalanche runnel, but at night it provided delightful Grade IV climbing, with a wee bit of V thrown in for interest. We needed to reach a corniced ridge for safety, but daybreak caught us high in the gully, and we were forced to traverse out over loose blocks to a narrow ledge, exposed to the sun and melting ice from above. We tried to go on during the next night. The idea was to set up a diagonal abseil to another gully to our left. Steve had disappeared round the corner, when I heard the crash and metallic chime of pegs and ice screws, and then a howl of pain, and a faint . . . "I'm all right, I think. But I can't see. My headtorch is broken." When I reached Steve, I could see that he had fallen about ten metres. He looked a mess, his glasses had been flattened against his face, the torch was dangling from his helmet, and he was bleeding copiously from a gash on the forehead.

"Can you help me with my glasses and torch, Victor?"

"Not just yet, let me get the camera out first, you look like a first-class mess."

"You . . . [unprintable reply] . . ."

The next morning Steve remembered a dream for the first time for years: he and Julian were climbing together on a steep scree slope. Steve had a fall and was dead physically, but still conscious. He could not remember what happened next, but it was not unpleasant he said.

Now we were going to try to climb an alternative line. The new line looked long, but seemed to avoid the worst of the séracs. It began with 1500 metres of broad couloirs in the shape of a giant "Z". After the Zeds there was the Pocket Glacier, a tiny hanging glacier like the top tier of a wedding cake, completely edged with ice cliffs. To

Paddy fields in the lower Arun valley on the walk-in to Makalu.

Andy, one of life's natural enthusiasts, in the snow entrance of our two-man tent.

Sustad positively enjoyed night climbing.

The formidable West Face of Makalu. The blank granite wall in the centre begins at around 7600 metres and is the size of Half Dome. I never saw snow settle on it.

The West Face of Kangchungtse. To avoid the stonefall which had repulsed all other attempts, we picked a line up the central snowfield. (UJ)

Ultar at 7388 metres was one of the highest unclimbed mountains in the world. Our line would be on the Hidden Pillar which drops almost 4000 metres from the summit, slightly right of centre.

Day One on the Hidden Pillar, Sustad leading.

Fowler and Crags made the first ascent of Hunza Peak (6250 metres) after climbing Bublimiting, the spire to the left.

A gotsil repair team above Hametabad.

The end of the Granite Traverse which had proved to be a delightful surprise, if a somewhat exposed one.

Peaks of the Panch Chuli massif emerge from the monsoon.

The tiger-striped fields near Balati on the way to the Dribbling Snout.

Venables on the summit of Rajrambha.

Threading a way through the Maze Glacier below Panch Chuli V.

Dick Renshawe belaying during the ascent of Panch Chuli V. It was from this point that Venables was to fall twenty-four hours later.

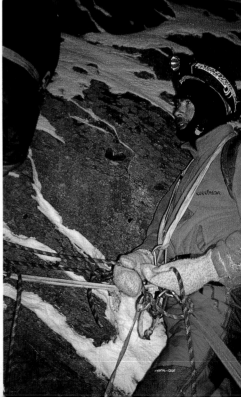

High above the entrance to the cwm was a lone sérac (above). Bonington and Sustad traverse cautiously under it (below: CB).

Accident on Panch Chuli, clockwise from top left: I help Stephen on the first lower by Dick down the steep slope (DR); Stephen grits his teeth; Dick takes over protecting Stephen's shattered legs as I lower (CB); the amazing helicopter pick up at 5600 metres (DR).

the left of the Pocket Glacier, the V Icefield led in 450 metres to a junction with the Triangular Icefield. Here the features were defined by granite cliffs. The Triangular Icefield would lead, we hoped, to the East Ridge and an easy but long walk to the summit.

That day it rained almost the whole day, big black clouds dwelt on Ultar. The next day it cleared a little in the afternoon, but more localised Ultar storms settled on the valley after that and lasted two days. Then the rain eased off, Steve called it dithering weather. I began feeling equivocal about the weather.

"I'd like it to clear up so I can dry my clothes, but then again, I'd like it to remain bad, so I don't feel too awful about not being on the hill."

"Trouble with you Catholics, you're only motivated by guilt."

At midnight on 31 August, we had packed for our final, ultimate, last-ditch attempt to force a new route up Ultar. We had eaten a spoonful of Grapenuts for breakfast, then watched the stars wink out one by one, as an enormous black shadow engulfed the sky.

While waiting for the tea to brew, Steve read by torchlight, absorbed in *The World According to Garp*. "Halepino smoked shrimp, seared, and placed on a bed of black bean and garlic sauce . . . with cucumber dill soup . . ." he read out.

"Stop, stop!" I was choking on a Grapenut. The water boiled, we packed away the tiny tent while scalding ourselves with the tea. Our sacks bulged out sideways, then it began to rain. We re-erected our minuscule tent, a Gore-tex Gemini with as much space as the underside of a British Rail dining table. It sounded like someone was playing a fire-hydrant on our tent. It sounded like the entire Hidden Valley would turn into a lake overnight. It sounded depressing. The rain continued over a second breakfast. But this time, in order to conserve our precious hill food, we dined on hot water and boiled wild rhubarb. Because of the food we would have to start up the mountain in the evening, or abandon the climb altogether. There was nothing else for it, we only had climbing food left. As the day wore on the rain faded into drizzle which drifted down the glacier and into the Hunza Valley beyond, leaving a freshly scrubbed sky and a glistening landscape.

Somewhere above the Ultar nullah, Mick and Crags were trying to complete the Hasegawa Route on the South Ridge.

We left our campsite at 8.00 p.m., dusk, and almost immediately became lost in the boulder scree. With only a pencil-thin beam of torchlight, night climbing can be very confusing.

"Your sack looks like you are carrying a drunk," said Steve, and it was true, it hung crazily sideways. Our rucksacks, filled with seven days' food, gear for forty or fifty abseils, ropes, tent, stove, sleeping bags and clothes for the minus 20 centigrade we expected during the nights, weighed over fifty pounds. At forty per cent of my body weight, this was far more than I or Steve wanted to carry, but we had already thrown out what we could. Water-bottles, toothbrush, spare food, sun cream (we could make do with lip cream) and, worst of all for Sustad, the last two chapters of *Moby Dick*, which he had torn out of Melville to reread. We didn't dare throw out any more food, seven days was not too generous for 3500 metres of climbing.

In order to avoid the wall that marathon runners hit, we stopped every three hours for a brew of melted ice, and some sweets. After the second brew, the moonless night and thin torchlight led us into the wrong couloir. We were forced to retreat from the blank granite wall, abseiling down two pitches before we could regain the correct line. It took us fourteen hours in all to reach our intended bivouac site, perched on top of a pocket-size hanging glacier. The last two hours were a form of purgatory unique to the Himalaya – being caught out in the sun on ice. We had 150 metres of hard ice to traverse, not steep, but so hard and brittle only the tips, about five millimetres, of our axes and crampons could penetrate the surface. This was the First Brittle Ice Traverse. We had to pitch it. It was horribly precarious, and on top of it all was the sun which, stripped of its protective layer of atmosphere, seemed to consist mainly of harmful rays: Ultra Violet Rays, Infra Red Rays, Microwave Rays, X Rays, Cosmic Rays, Cook-em-Alive Rays and Boil-in-Your-Skin Rays. Under the Geneva Convention, Himalayan Climbing would certainly be illegal. It is so hot at these lower altitudes that even without the avalanches and rockfall, you have to climb at night until you are over 6500 metres. There was another problem with the heat: we couldn't sleep. Baking in the tent, we listened to the mountain around us growling as small icebergs detached themselves, pounding a path to the nearest glacier.

At the Pocket Glacier, we ate one day's hill food, and stashed another: a small packet of instant mash, a tiny wedge of cheese, a clove of garlic, a vegetable stock cube and watery drinking chocolate. About 1500 kilocalories in all. It is estimated that climbers can consume up to 8000 kcal per day, and we knew from past experience (this proves you never learn from your mistakes) that we would lose about a kilogram in body weight for each day on the hill.

That night we started on the next section of our route, traversing left along the top of our Pocket Glacier, under 1200-metre granite cliffs to a "V"-shaped icefield, guarded at its base by a large berg-schrund, which had fanglike icicles drooling from its upper lip. The minute we reached that bergschrund, there was a sound like a Volkswagen Beetle, followed by a dull thud.

"Waaaatchout, Steve . . . Stonefall!"

"I know, let's get on with it," came the reply out of the dark. Damned laconic, I thought. One good thing about fear, though, my feet, which had been icy cold, were now experiencing a delicious liquid flow of lukewarm blood.

On the southern horizon, there was a flickering light, either St Elmo's fire, or the border war had broken out again. Steve decided it must be the latter. The flickering recurred over the next two nights, so he was probably right, though I had read that powder-snow avalanches can produce a shock of static electricity. I pulled my hood over my helmet and we went on.

Climbing through the bergschrund required our full concentration. We had been moving together, but now we started pitching it. The initial steep ice was followed by near-vertical sections of heavily verglassed rock. Occasional pebbles or small icicles whistled and tinkled as they missed us in the eerie darkness. This was exciting, we worked in little pools of headtorch light, thinking "Now this is why we are really here." Steep, difficult and mind-absorbing climbing. Problems. How to pass this overhang? How to protect that balancing act? Will a knifeblade in this hairline crack do? A fat nut behind the flake? It looks properly frozen in. Our route followed the left fork of the "V" icefield, always moving left towards the summit. The final pitches of the icefield brought more of that ghastly brittle ice, the Second Brittle Ice Traverse. Again the sun caught us, and it also dawned on us that we were tired, lead-limbed. Steve offered me a sweet to raise the blood-sugar level, and we stopped to contemplate our position.

"Magnificent, Steve, eh?"

"Guess we must be eight or nine thousand feet above the glacier. Can you see which way the route goes?"

Always the same question, which way, and how hard? This time we were too high. The line we had identified through the binoculars was 100 metres beneath us, and we were faced with a 60-metre traverse across a steep granite cliff, on the other side of which lay our next objective, the Triangular Icefield. The granite traverse, in spite of being in the sun, turned out to be a delightful surprise. Huge, bucket-like holds, and a yawning abyss below our feet sweeping away to the glacier. Rust Red Rock, Wedgwood Sky, Paper White

Snow. The climber's version of sunbathing on the Costa Blanca. A
Third Brittle Ice Traverse led to a fine bivouac site under a small ice
cliff on the Great Triangular Icefield, where we spent the rest of the
day hiding from the sun, sleeping bags draped over the tiny tent to
block out the sun's rays, and making thin brews of packet vegetable
soup where the orange and green bits had failed to rehydrate.

We were now one night's work from the summit ridge. Our line would
follow the Triangular Icefield, a feature at about 50 degrees, dotted
with ice cliffs, its apex 450 metres higher. The top of the Icefield was
connected to the Summit Ridge by a double-corniced snow crest, about
150 metres long, leading to 60 metres of difficult climbing, which in turn
led to a col on the Summit Ridge at slightly over 6700 metres. From
this col we could see easy snow slopes to the summit at 7300 metres.
We felt optimistic about the weather, which had remained perfect, and
about our chances. But our optimism was horribly misplaced. By 11.00
a.m. the next morning, we knew our climb was over. Not only that, we
would be lucky to make it down alive.

Steve and I had climbed to the end of the Double Corniced Crest,
which looked like whipped ice cream, looping over itself in white curls.
It looked, as Fowler would have said, cuddly. As we clambered onto
it, we recognised the crest for what it really was, hateful and difficult,
with all the solidity of a haystack on edge, balanced on a skyscraper.
Steve led out a rope-length, spent an hour on it then retreated. He had
been crawling over the curls. Could I see an easier way to avoid this?

"What's the problem?"

"The mushrooms . . . it's interesting but awful. Very rare to find
snow, not soft but rotten to a depth of five feet or more. Bottomless
rot, don't know what to do about it. To put the snow stake all the
way in and still have it rip out in your hands."

"If you find this interesting, you'll love Hastings. Can you crawl
under that first mushroom, and out onto the ice below?"

"I'll try."

When it came to my turn to lead through, the conditions were every
bit as miserable as Steve had made out, with three-metre balloons of
soft snow overhanging crumbling ice. There were no conventional
runners, that goes without saying. But crossing the crest brought the
rope zig-zagging around the mushrooms.

I battled with the rucksack for control of gravity, me leaning out
one way and the sack, deciding to follow an independent line, leaning
the other. I managed to persuade the sack to follow a peculiar move
over a wave of snow; I had reached an impasse traversing the rotten

ice beneath the crest of the wave. The next mushroom billowed out like a spinnaker. The only thing to do was to cross to the other side. The sun had now reached us, and begun to add to our discomfort. Reaching up with an ice axe, I found I was able to lay my arm on the crest. I could not pull, of course, there was no resistance in the snow. Instead it was necessary to lay the other arm on top of the crest as well, and execute a mole-like movement of the head, pushing through the snow nose first. A great blob was stuck to my face as I lay doubled over my arms, feet kicking out in space behind, while I tried to shake myself free of this unwelcome nosebag.

The next thing was to try and get astride the crest. But I was breathless with even the tiniest movement, without hauling myself and the reluctant sack onto this roof ridge. The sun didn't help. Sitting astride, wheezing gently as I caught my breath, I saw a wall of dry rot shouldering up to the next over-sailing ice-cream. Was that the way? A scrape at the surface produced a deep groove. A scrape at the groove produced a deeper groove. Below the crest the rotten sun-baked snow fell steeply and disappeared. Parallax showed that the snow, when it reappeared, was hundreds of metres lower. Red outcrops at the edge of the cliff hinted at the nature of the abyss and the unseen granite wall. Looking up, the crest ran into large buttresses, but a gully to our left led to the Summit Ridge in a very few pitches. This ice-cream snow was not going to stop us. Wearily hauling myself up onto the roof-ridge, I attacked the dry rot with both arms and legs flailing. After a few minutes, I found, to my surprise, that I had made upward movement. I was at the top of a shallow vertical trench up to the armpits.

Steve was in the lead on the fourth Brittle Ice Thing, when I noticed that my left crampon had broken. We had a discussion at rope length, me shouting, and Steve hollerin'. We agreed to push on. Within five minutes Steve hollered again that his ice hammer had broken. In all our combined climbing careers, spanning a total of twenty-seven years, neither of us had broken an axe or crampon before. Now, within the space of five minutes, we had broken one each. It was unbelievable. We were one day from the summit, after six weeks of effort. The sun shone out of a mockingly blue sky. I could have cried had our situation not been so serious. Now we had to reverse all those Brittle Ice Traverses with broken tools. It took us the rest of the day to struggle back to our last bivouac.

We lay in the tent exhausted and depressed. The day passed slowly. Steve's Troll helmet, like Arnolphini's mirror, made a fish-eye lens for the tent, reflecting everything in its orb. I remembered how Stephen Venables had dropped his rucksack, our stove, and tent poles at 7000 metres on Rimo I, and knew how the poor fellow felt. Devastated. I had caught him jumping up and down, tearing at his hair, and wailing, "Why me? Oh, why me?" And now I felt like doing the same. So did Sustad, which just shows that Norwegian-Americans are not totally devoid of emotion. We spent the day preparing our abseil equipment, attaching short slings to our ice screws and pegs. We planned to cut ice bollards and ice threads to save our precious supply of abseil gear. There was 2500 metres of descent to the glacier to prepare for. The Hunza river flowed 4500 metres below us; edging it, like fine purfling, the Karakoram Highway. A patchwork of green terraces, bordering the river, betrayed the cultivation of Hametabad.

"It's horrible being able to see Hametabad from here," said Steve. "It would be much better not being able to see anything."

And the backache! At first we thought it was the sheer weight of the rucksacks, but now we believed it must have been the tent, you just could not sit up straight at any time. Everything had to be done hunched over.

Before starting the long retreat, we waited till dark, for the sun to go off the slopes, for the stones and avalanche slopes to refreeze, and possibly because the sight was too horrible to contemplate. The sound turned out to be worse. No moon. Soot-black night. As I dangled in the middle of our first abseil, there was a sound like a freight train out of a tunnel, as a large section of mountainside decided to share our icefield. In the echo of the receding explosions, and the sulphurous cordite of the rock fall, I said to Steve we might live longer if we abseiled down the rocky left side of the icefield, well away from the fall line.

"You're right, if we stay here we are going to maybe die."

On the rocky left side, our ropes immediately jammed. It was Steve's turn to retrieve them. With heart in mouth, he pulled tight on the free end; it would not move. He was not tied into the belay, he could not be, the other end of the rope was somewhere up there in the blackness. He pulled again, there was no movement. I shone my torch at him and he made a face like he had just chewed a lemon.

"I am going to have to pull from higher up . . . I guess it's the knot . . ." I nodded.

Steve climbed up to free the end of the rope, crampons splintering the ice and sparking on the rock, mitts and gloves fumbling in the cold. Steve only ever swore when frightened, and he had begun swearing copiously. "This effing rope . . . watch me carefully, Vic." He had also developed an exasperated "Urrrgh" grunt like the parent of a naughty child. This appeared to be reserved for any piece of equipment that failed to respond to his wishes. Interesting noise; I wondered if he got it from his father. He went up, "Urrrgh . . . effing rope . . . urrrrgh."

"Take care," I said impotently, making plans to try and grab him should he fall in my general direction. Steve was up there for half an hour, while I shivered with cold and neurosis.

"Victor," came the voice from the dark, "if the ropes go on jamming like this we are going to definitely die. If we abseil down the middle of the face, we'll only maybe die."

"That is incontrovertible logic," I said to myself.

In the middle of the icefield, there was a waterfall in a large runnel. The nearest thing I had seen to this were the monsoon drains we used to have in Malaya, deep concrete channels meant to take away storm water, but which usually lay like man-traps, just under the flood surface. The ropes took the first opportunity of falling into the waterfall, and freezing solid, bending at unpredictable angles, and more or less imitating wire hawser. Some hours later, I don't know how many, two abysmal and free-hanging abseils deposited us below the fangs of the bergschrund. We were not far from the Pocket Glacier, where we stopped for two hours before pushing on to make the most of the night. The imperative was, as always, to make as much ground as possible before the sun made all progress impossibly dangerous. Against this we had to set our growing exhaustion, and increasingly dysfunctional limbs.

Steve, with the instinct that marks him out as a real mountaineer, and not just a climber, had searched for and seen an abseil that avoided the First Brittle Ice Traverse. It took us past the Pocket Glacier séracs, where the ropes twisted into corkscrews and jammed tight.

"I can't believe this," said Steve, as I clambered up the free end. "These are the worst jamming ropes I've ever used. There should be a public health warning on each one."

They jammed up just one more time, as we were passing under a particularly nasty-looking sérac. It was Steve's turn to free the end once more:

"Urrrgh . . . effing rope . . . urrrgh!"

The sun emerged into an almost clear sky as we reached the top of the "Z" couloirs. The Hidden Valley was spread out before us like a model landscape. It was incredibly, and compellingly, beautiful. In that moment a realisation dawned on me.

We weren't unlucky at all. We were privileged just to be here. To have attempted two new routes from this valley. To have explored this unvisited glacier. My mood changed from one of deep despair to sheer exultation. Probably it was also the knowledge that we might now survive the descent, but I shouted to Steve:

"Hey, Steve . . . wouldn't you rather have failed on this route, than have succeeded on the Japanese Route?"

After a moment came the reply: "Yeah . . . every time."

We found the "Z"s were now made of deep porridge, but at least we could walk down facing out, sliding and glissading in crampons, down to the glacier, where we paused to don the rope before crossing the slots. We crossed the bergschrund, followed by a flock of sun-loosened stones, over the avalanche debris, then the pebble-pimpled hard ice where bits of broken sérac lay like building blocks. We descended the glacier covered with black stones, down the scree and turf, tired and tripping over the crampons. We drank water from the spring, we were back onto the moraine. There was the rock from which the ibex mother and child had watched us, around the Island of Pinnacles pointing meaningfully skywards.

Julian had left us a tin of tuna and a packet of macaroni. Sustad said, "What a team player, heart of gold in spite of being an aristo."

It was a long and disheartening climb back through the Pass of the Shifting Stones. On the third col, I saw a small iridescent blue bird, and turned to point it out to Steve, who said, "Look out," soon followed by "You idiot!" as I missed the next boulder and went head-first down the boulder scree.

When I stopped sliding, my arms and legs had been scraped raw. "It'll go well with that gash on your head," I said. We were so tired that Steve said the last time he'd he'd seen us so clumsy was leaving the Nobody Inn.

"We failed," Steve said to Kees when we returned to our Supernova at Shokumshun.

"So did Mick and Crags," replied Kees, "and the other news is the Japanese are here. There are ten of them. They've taken 130 porters up the Ultar Gorge, and what is more, they have brought 6800 metres of Kevlar rope for fixing."

"This is mind-boggling," I thought, as I looked over our Base Camp with its two tents, brought up with the help of our four porters. A week earlier Steve and I had been on our way to the summit of Ultar with a pair of 50-metre nylon ropes, and no more gear than we could carry.

Chapter Fourteen

In the Shimshal Pamirs

It was mid-September. The team had gone. Kees had a filming project which I was to record the sound for. This was a documentary about the Karakoram Highway, to be screened on Channel Four. Our job was to walk up to the remote village of Shimshal, and then film all the night stops, chai houses and repair shops down the Highway. Paul Cleary, the film's producer, was going to shoot all the daytime stuff. This was good. I'd not had the opportunity to visit Shimshal before.

The walk to Shimshal started opposite the snout of the Batura Glacier, on the true left bank of the Hunza river. We had four porters with us to carry Kees' tripods, his camera, the 16 mm Aaton, food and tents. The idea was to film the walk-in using our porters as a demonstration of how remote the village was.

So Kees set up the tripod behind a sand dune to film the men sauntering round the corner. When they saw him they suddenly realised they were on film and began to walk with funereal dignity. At which point Kees leapt up and shouted, "Walk normally! Walk normally!", waving his arms. "Faster! Faster!" The men broke into a jog. Kees waved both arms maniacally, the men waved their arms in imitation, and began leaping up and down like Kees. "*No, no, walk!*" They slowed down to a creep once more. "Please, just act yourselves," Kees pleaded at the top of his voice. The men stopped in confusion and began chattering among themselves, casting several suspicious glances at Kees. This performance was repeated at regular intervals for three days up and the two days back.

With no road, everything had to be portered in over a desert landscape. Mostly it looked like Arizona, the Hollywood badlands.

There was no indication of greenery, and it was marvellous to think that any community would have found a valley so far from any reasonable water supply.

The Aaton began to suffer from the cold, and sometimes stopped working for no apparent reason. On these occasions Kees made the whole party stop, while he lit the gas stove and warmed the camera over the flames. At other times he stroked the Aaton with his scarf or other soft things. He talked to it a lot, and at night he slept with the camera cuddled up to him like a teddy bear.

On the third day we met the only other person on the path, a dusty young man carrying a large bundle of wood. He had just left Shimshal, and spoke excellent English. The wood was for the camp of Zyarat which had no other fuel. He would complete the walk in a day and a half.

"Are you going to Pasu?"

"No, I am going to Canada."

"Canada? I can't remember any village called Canada, can you, Kees?"

"No," said Kees. "Is it near Pasu?"

"You don't know Canada?" asked the villager. "It is just north of the USA." He looked closely at us. Then explained very slowly, in simple words, that he was going to the Aga Khan college in Montreal."

"Excuse me," said Kees, "I'll just see if I can persuade the Aaton to film you," and he got out the gas stove and began talking to the camera.

The standard of education in Shimshal was higher than anywhere outside the Hunza valley with ninety-five per cent literacy among twelve-year-olds. The head teacher, one of Shimshal's spiritual leaders, was called Daulat Amin. There was no electricity, not even hydro power, in this village, and though they had once been given a radio set by a Japanese expedition, because they were so close to the border, the government refused to allow them to use the set. Not even for medical purposes. When we got there the village appeared to be empty. "They are in the pamirs," said Daulat. Seeing our confusion he went on, "*Pamir* is how we say pastures." Of course! The language here was Whaki, the dialect of Persian centred in the Whakan Corridor. Pamir carries exactly the same meaning as alp. High pasture. In fact, the only newspapers in the language had to be smuggled across the border from the Soviet Union.

Up in the pamir the families tended their yaks. Daulat Amin told us about the yaks crossing the rivers. "They are very fond of it when they are crossing the rivers. They are getting very happy. Because it is nature's gift, for the people of Shimshal for travelling."

After Shimshal, Kees and I went back briefly to Karimabad to visit the Japanese team before filming the nightlife of the Highway. It was now the end of September. Hasegawa had established his Camp 3, at around 6000 metres on his 1990 route. Tsuneo Hasegawa, the leader, was still on the mountain, but his Base Camp manager was there. It was his wife, Masami. She smiled as she poured out the tiny bowls of green tea. We were in the dining tent. Low table, cushions to sit cross legged at. All very traditional.

The Hasegawa team decided to use, I was going to say large quantities of fixed rope, but the adjective doesn't go far enough. They took 6800 metres, that is over 22,000 feet, of Kevlar. Kevlar is stronger and lighter than nylon. This was to enable them to cross and recross not only difficult but also dangerous ground in apparent safety. I had expected to be hypercritical. Their methods would almost certainly give them the edge over us. To the Japanese that was all that was needed to justify the use of fixed ropes and all the other paraphernalia of ante-diluvian tactics. They just could not see that siege expeditions belong to the dustbin of history. As for climbing ultra-light, they thought we were just very odd. But I left with mixed feelings. The thing is, they were so enthusiastic, they were happy, human. As I left, I wished them luck and a safe return. I was sure they would manage the latter with all that fixed rope. For the moment, however, they were being delayed because it had been snowing for ten days.

Kees and I sipped our bowls of green tea. The walkie-talkie crackled into life, Masami San got up to speak to her husband. She told him we were there and he referred to events eleven years before on Uzum Brakk, or Conway's Ogre, when we had rescued the Japanese climbers, Omiya and Okano. "Tsuneo say thank you for rescue Omiya. Omiya, good friend!" She smiled again.

The rays were without heat or warmth. It was an English sun, an autumn sun. It lit our sitting room. It had taken me three weeks to face the job of unpacking. As I shook my clothes from the rucksack, shafts of gold, diagonal columns of Gilgit dust, pierced the cool gloom. On the table a white porcelain doric candle holder held the last gutterings of a red candle. A torn page lay beside the candle. The phone message read:

> Tsuneo Hasegawa and Kiyotaka Hoshino died on 10th October, Avalanche, Ultar. Cremated and buried by Mrs Hasegawa at Karimabad.

I looked at a slide of Mrs Hasegawa, Masami San, smiling as Kees pointed the camera in the Japanese dining tent with the low table, and tiny bowls of green tea, and remembered the crackle of the radio as the Hasegawas talked about the rescue of Omiya. She smiled out of the photograph. There had been no one to rescue Tsuneo. Masami Hasegawa was their Base Camp manager. So she buried her husband. Death is not about statistics, it's about the people who are left behind.

I was surrounded by half-unpacked rucksacks and expedition gear. The sitting room looked a mess. I looked at the crumpled note and reread it, trying to work out in my mind something which I suspect is incapable of comprehension. I screwed up the note and tore it, twisting and crushing it, then I threw it in the bin.

There was a distant howl. A small child stubbed his toe, fell over the steps, or did some temporarily painful thing to himself in the neighbouring garden.

I'd been back three weeks. Islington was just returning to its comfortable familiarity. I didn't know why, but it seemed to take me for ever to return to earth from these trips. Maggie and Hugo had already gone to Kew. I was alone in the house. I couldn't write, so was easily distracted. The phone rang; it was Julian. He'd been back a month, and wanted slides.

"Got a couple of lectures, old boy."

"I hear you've been working on the extension."

"Yes, I've got the foundations all dug, took a day with the JCB."

"What about your doric columns?" He had acquired these from the ruins of a Paladian country house.

"Oh, yes, fine fellows, moved them. Brought in the timber crane for the morning, what?"

"I am coming up next week, you around?"

"No, I'm orf to shoot a few defenceless birds. Scotland, y'know."

A few minutes later the phone rang again.

"Er, yes?"

"Ah, Slippery! Apparently we've got to do a lecture in Wales."

"Michael, how wonderful to hear from you. How is the Civil Service, still there I take it?"

"Victor, you're changing the subject again . . ."

I walked the hundred yards to our corner shop on Newington Green. The whitewashed door and window surrounds glowed paper white, against the dirty London stocks. These yellow bricks, weathered into dreary browns, lined our street as well as half the rest of Islington. "There should be a law against using London stocks in London," the architect in me pronounced out loud. A startled old woman with a dirty brown overcoat looked up sharply, and crossed to the other side of the road. Her suspicious stare followed me down the street.

A month earlier I had been shuffling in the Hunza dust, collecting breakfast from the Mountain Refuge. It had been the same sun. I shivered and pulled the fibre pile closer round me as I recited . . . milk, eggs, washing-up liquid and butter. At the shop Mahmoud and Moody were all smiles and broke into Urdu.

"Kie al a hai?"

"Achha, achha."

Moody got his name from the past. He used to scowl at his customers. He used to open his shop from 7.00 a.m. to 8.00 p.m. every day. He wasn't just grumpy in the mornings, he was grumpy all day long, and just had the usual things a corner shop has. Pretty expensive too, I thought. If you asked for, say, real Soya sauce, he'd retort gruffly that nobody would buy it. "The customer is always right!" was his way of finishing off a conversation he did not like. One day, inexplicably, he began to change: he started to stock almost anything that his customers asked for, or even mentioned in passing. He hired a smiling assistant, Mahmoud, and we found Moody had a name, Ramesh. The shop hours became shorter. Ramesh grew more and more affable. The battered old Volvo that used to live outside the shop changed one day into a new one. Now he doesn't open on Sundays at all. And he smiles all the time . . . "Customer is always right," but there is still a challenging glint in his eye when he says this.

My supply of Urdu was now fully exhausted. And my memory. As usual I came away without the washing-up liquid. I was still in Hunza seeing dark shadows over ravines, the gotsil dripping water and trailing vegetation like a hanging garden, to the distant sound of children singing.

PART THREE

PANCH CHULI

1992

The Panch Chuli massif lies geographically between Nanda Devi in Garhwal and Api in Nepal. The highest peak of the massif is Panch Chuli II (6904m), Panch Chuli I being an insignificant pimple on its side. The other striking peaks of the massif are, from west to east, Rajrambha (6537m), Nagalaphu (6410m), the superb Sahadev (5782m), Panch Chuli III (6312m), Panch Chuli IV (6334m), Panch Chuli V (6437m), Telkot (6102m), Bainti (6071m) and Nagling (6041m).

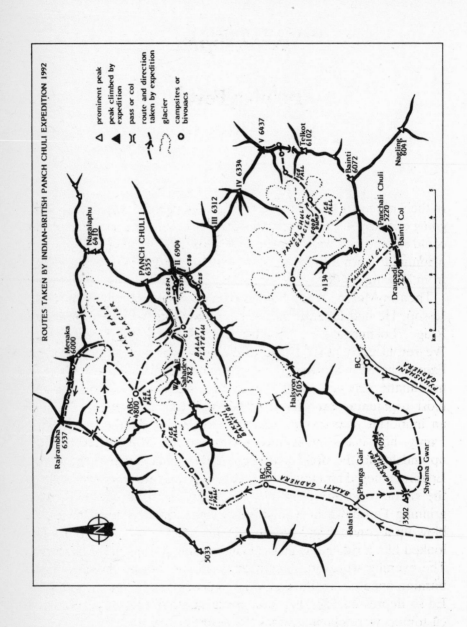

ROUTES TAKEN BY INDIAN–BRITISH PANCH CHULI EXPEDITION 1992

△ prominent peak
▲ peak climbed by expedition
⋈ pass or col
↑ route and direction taken by expedition
〜 glacier
○ campsites or bivouacs

Chapter Fifteen

Bombay Fever

In the winter of 1991–2 I was reconsidering my life. Architecture was going one way, I was trying to go another. To put it romantically you could say the hills were beckoning. To put it less romantically, I was planning to earn a living on them, and was on the verge of moving from Newington Green to Scotland.

Then in March, Andy Fanshawe died while climbing with Ulric Jessop. He had fallen from the penultimate belay stance on Eagle Ridge, Lochnagar. Ed Douglas and I were in the Nobody Inn. We retold each other all the old Fanny stories. Ed had lived in Fanny's house in Stockport; the stories poured out. We remembered his lunatic driving. Jim Fotheringham had once said it was the most frightening experience of his life, and he's a dentist! I had an immortal memory of drinking Stolichnaya by the bottle with Fanny, how it had all seemed under control till we tried to stand up and found the brain had become disconnected from the body. Ed remembered him bounding up rock climbs, his style representing the victory of enthusiasm over technique. I produced a slide of a grinning Fanshawe in Kathmandu. Somehow he had managed to blow up a condom and pull it over his head at the same time. He looked like a ridiculous guardsman wearing a translucent bearskin. The evening wore on, and through all the stories shone Fanny's burning appetite for life. And now he was dead. I had never seen Ed so depressed. The PA announced another trivial question, the customers were playing games. I wanted to cry.

With a move north in mind I had already started lining myself up for the Association of British Mountain Guides qualifications a couple of years before. It was just that expeditions would keep getting in the way. My mind went back to spring 1990 when the intention was all shiny new. I wanted to climb with Jim Fotheringham for the day, to relive old memories perhaps, but Jim was going to climb with Chris Bonington. "Why don't you join us?" said Jim. "Chris won't mind. He may be hairy, but he doesn't bite."

So I did join them. It was wet. Sustad had warned me, he'd lived for six months in the Lakes, and it was always blustery and rain-soaked. So we would be doing easy climbs in bad weather, the traditional resort of ageing mountaineers. Rock athletes wouldn't dream of going out in the rain. They'd rather spend their time training on the climbing walls. Sometimes, when I remember to think of it, so would I. But not this day. I had to get used to the Lakes, where the entry level test for the ABMG was to be held. In fact the first part of the test was the next day.

Debbie Fotheringham had made cling-filmed sandwiches, two each for Jim, Chris, and me. We sipped from flasks of coffee. Watched the downpour fade to a drizzle. Water trickled in a little stream from the hem of my jacket, down the overtrousers and into my wet leather boots. High in the air a pair of falcons were quartering the sky. Jim turned to me with his uniquely mischievous grin.

"Which way now, Victor?"

I stared blankly at the guide book. It wasn't at all obvious. We were sitting in the back of a small cave. Yet the route description didn't suggest leaving. Chris, who had done the climb before, couldn't remember either. Jim believes that Climbing Is Not Competitive. So he waited just that fraction of a second longer to confirm to himself that we were indeed lost before setting off.

"Come on, it's easy," he said, disappearing like the Mad Hatter. A few minutes later he popped out of the cliff fifteen metres above us. Chris followed the cave pitch, and resurfaced into the drizzle to find the Hatter had disappeared up the next pitch. I followed Chris. The finish came suddenly and presented us with a walk off to the left, or a boulder problem up a slabby groove. The Mad Hatter ignored the groove. Chris retreated from it half-way. He said it was too wet and greasy. This I could not resist, even though Climbing Is Not Competitive. I reached Chris's high point and began to have uneasy thoughts. Some bastard had definitely covered the holds in Vaseline. I looked down. Three metres to a big ledge. Worst that could happen would be a broken ankle, I reasoned. I was right. Not long after, there was a slithering and a loud snapping crack. Like glove puppets, the two faces popped over the top. One smooth and blond, one hairy and russet.

"Be a'right in a min." I gestured at my boot which was now pointing sideways. "Just twisted it a bit."

Jim, dentist by profession and therefore a great expert on feet, said he thought it looked worse than that, but didn't offer to carry my sack.

"I'll be OK," I insisted. "I've got to be. The Guides test starts tomorrow morning."

I don't know what Chris thought, but I like to think he was genuinely concerned and sincere when he said it was something that could happen to anybody and that risk was an essential part of climbing anyway. Nice man. I hopped uphill to clear the top of the crag. An unpleasant grinding noise, such as my car often makes, accompanied me. Near the top of the cliff Chris and Jim were deeply engrossed on a small ledge. As I hobbled closer I could see a sheep's tail sticking out from the huddle.

How disgusting, I thought.

"Needs rescuing," they said. Of course it does, I thought. It needs rescuing from you two. The animal had jumped down to a ledge the size of a small bed. The grass had by now been eaten all up, and it could not make the jump back up, but down was forty-five metres.

"Pass me your harness," Jim said to Chris.

"I'll try to creep around its back, slip the harness over it and we can haul it up."

"I don't think this is a good idea," said Chris, getting the rope out. I had to agree with him. I had in mind the famous sheep rescue at Cummingston when the tide had cut off a sheep, and the rescuers had hauled it up by a waist line, which had somehow slipped. The farmer's face was an awful sight when he saw that the line had become a noose, swinging his once magnificent prize-winning animal by its neck.

I continued downhill. Soon I had to sit every five or six hops. Voices drifted on the breeze.

"I can't get round its back, it keeps turning to face me." Sensible animal, I thought.

"I don't think the farmer would like this . . . what if the sheep decides to jump?"

So it might, so it might, I thought to myself. I certainly would.

"It's OK, I'll try getting round it the other way, then change direction. Perhaps I can surprise it with the harness. Can you belay both of us?"

Spring had arrived that weekend. I hopped onto a small yellow flower, and ground it out of existence. A squeal tore the air as the two falcons we had seen earlier began to harry a passing pigeon.

In the background the breeze-wafted voices continued. "Damned beast keeps turning to face me . . . Perhaps it doesn't trust you, Jim . . . Chris can you *please* attract its attention so I can get behind it . . ."

Exhausted by the hopping descent, I collapsed on a mossy stream bank. The peregrine falcons had struck their quarry, which spun to earth leaving a trail of feathers. The pigeon landed by a large boulder. The falcons spiralled down for the kill, describing an elegant double helix. Their intentions were not lost on the pigeon, which immediately popped down a rabbit hole conveniently located under the boulder. By now I was too far away to hear more than the odd phrase from Jim and Chris.

"It's standing on the rope . . . *Whistle* at it or something . . . It doesn't look happy . . . Gerrit off that rope . . ."

Perhaps, I thought, if I dunked the foot in the stream, it might get the swelling down for the morning. Unrolling the socks revealed a monstrously swollen joint, the size of a ham.

The peregrines had landed and were stalking round the boulder. They were clearly nervous. Odd to see these soaring birds of prey look anxious and uncomfortable. They kept looking over their shoulders, could barely bring themselves to remain aground long enough to poke their sharp beaks into the rabbit hole. But the pigeon had gone to ground.

Chris and Jim failed to rescue the sheep. The Mad Hatter was clearly disgruntled, the falcons took one look at him and flew off in a desperate hurry.

"What about the sheep?" I asked.

"We had to leave it, Chris's harness isn't big enough."

"Oh," I said. "Really? Well, lucky sheep, eh?"

"Pretty good melon you have there," said Jim, still not offering to carry my sack for the two-mile walk to the car.

"So," said Chris, "you are Victor Saunders. I think I'd better take you to hospital."

Oh great! I said to myself. The first time I meet the great man. He'll probably take me for a half-wit. But then again, anyone who is prepared to climb with that stark staring Fotheringham creature probably doesn't notice simple idiocy.

And that is how I met Christian Bonington.

A year after the sheep incident I was asked if I would like to be counted in on a joint Indo-British expedition being set up by Harish Kapadia and Chris. This would be the third of Harish's Indo-British ventures. I had been on the first in 1985 to Rimo. That expedition had accomplished a large number of firsts, including a classic piece of exploration, the first ascent of Rimo III by Jim Fotheringham and Dave Wilkinson. It was also the time when Venables dropped his rucksack at about 7000 metres just below the unclimbed summit of Rimo I. The second excursion, to Chong Kumdan in 1991, had put four climbers, including Dave Wilkinson again, on the highest unclimbed massif in India. Both these expeditions visited the Eastern Karakoram via Ladakh. For 1992 Harish chose the Kumaon Himalaya, that part of Uttar Pradesh just west of the Nepalese border, the general target being the Panch Chuli massif.

Wading through Harish's ever growing bundles of expedition reports and typewritten foolscap notes we discovered that this was a historically very interesting area, with visits from Hugh Ruttledge in 1929, and Bill Murray and Heinrich Harrer in the early fifties. Several Indian expeditions had visited Panch Chuli since then, and the first ascent of Panch Chuli II was achieved by the Indo-Tibetan Border Police in 1976. All parties said that bad weather seemed endemic to this region. Only Panch Chuli II and Rajrambha had been climbed, which left us with a treasure-chest of fine objectives.

In recent years the border regions of India have been closed to foreigners, the dreaded "Inner Line" marking off a corridor of some of the finest mountains in the Himalaya. The Inner Line was, of course, a British invention. For us, the way into this corridor was Harish's Joint Indo-British expedition. There is some sort of just karma in that. There were going to be six Western climbers in the party. The Mad Hatter had been part of Chris's original team, but when he couldn't come, Chris decided to pair up with Graham Little from Edinburgh. Stephen Venables and Dick Renshaw would make up another rope, while Sustad and I would make the third Western pair.

We drove to the Lakes in the Sustad-mobile, a battered and very

old Escort van, and, ears still ringing from the half-silenced diesel
engine, we listened as Chris deciphered and ordered the notes from
Bombay.

"These Manali men and Kumaonis . . . are they part of the
team?"

"Sort of, Harish tends to use the same base camp staff for all his
trips. They travel across the Himalaya to meet him. They do the
cooking, and the portering between camps. The Kumaonis Harish
had on Rimo were really good."

"We seemed to have five of them this time. And this Muslim
Contractor; that is a person, not a job, isn't it?"

"Yes, Chris, he was with us on Rimo. Good company too."

"Funny sort of name that, Muslim, don't you think?"

"Yes, indeed . . . Christian."

The day after we flew into Bombay I was ill. It was midday, I was
alone, feverish and stupefied by the heat. My throat was ablaze. I
needed a drink. The air was thick with moisture, and sweat rolled
from my neck and arms as I wondered where the entrance to the
restaurant was. I found myself in an alley under a pergola with
creepers and orange flowers which led round the peeling side of
the building to the elegant covered entrance of the Bombay Cricket
Club. The stadium itself looked slightly worse for wear. White paint
peeled from the back of the high stands. Moss and creeping weeds
were insinuating themselves into the cracks and would soon be fed
by the monsoon. But the entrance was set out with large-leafed
pot plants. Palm trees and magnolias had been gathered artfully
round the glass doors that led to an air-conditioned lobby and cool
dry air.

I wondered briefly how Harish had managed to install us in
the Cricket Club, but more immediately I wondered how long I
could stand this thirst. Probably there were fading black-and-white
photographs of great cricketers, but I was too ill to look up as I made
my way to the club restaurant. A waiter with white linen wrapped
round his head brought a steel jug of water and a glass which I filled
and added iodine to. The dim, badly lit restaurant was almost empty
except for a sinister party of civil servants discussing something in
hushed tones and glancing occasionally in my direction.

Harish had dropped off the invitation cards in the morning. On
one side was printed a programme, 4.00 p.m. to 5.30 p.m.: Stephen
Venables 'Ascent of Everest by Kangshung Face' – Story of the

epic solo climb of the face from China, without oxygen, in 1988. 5.30 p.m. to 7.30 p.m.: Chris Bonington, CBE 'Thirty Years of Mountaineering' – Climbing in the highest ranges of the world over the last three decades, covering difficult ascents, expeditions and various personalities.

"You must be there by three o'clock." Harish had glared at me for daring to be ill on such an important occasion. The glass floated before my face, I found myself tasting the iodine. Chris and Stephen were at the Godrej Industrial Estate preparing for the afternoon. Steve and Dick were in another part of Bombay packing the expedition supplies into gunny sacks for the train, presumably with the help of Muslim and Monesh. My job was to recuperate in time for the evening's entertainment. I turned over the card.

The invitation was issued by The Himalayan Club, represented by K.N. Naoroji, President, and the Godrej group of companies by S.P. Godrej, Chairman. "S.P." was a most unlikely industrial mogul. Quiet, modest, white haired and gentle. The Godrejs were a Parsee family, of course.

The card said the venue was the Patkar Hall. I would call a taxi presently and hope the driver knew the way. Meanwhile I wondered if I could force down a *paper dosa* or perhaps a small portion of idli sambar. The waiters ignored my feeble attempts at beckoning them, but a passing stranger threw a copy of the *Times of India* on the table. The opened middle pages announced a Bombay-wide transport strike. The Shiv Sena (not followers of the god Shiva, but named after the leader of the great Maharashtran revolt against Mogul rule), were organising the strike to obtain irrigation rights for the rural communities. Nothing would run. Any private cars daft enough to venture onto the streets would be stoned. Presumably that included taxis.

I wondered how I would make the lecture. I abandoned my attempts at obtaining food and staggered off back into the sun and heat, where I was almost run over by a stampede of taxis. "Oh, well," I thought, as I climbed out of the pavement and into a superheated tin box taxi.

The Patkar Hall was stuffed full of dignitaries. Through the pain in my chest and roaring temperature I felt an odd sensation which I could not first place. Turbaned waiters in red jackets brought canapés on silver trays. One tray held a phalanx of thin-stemmed glasses half filled with clear straw-coloured and slightly fizzing drinks. I was burning up and took two. I began to understand the sensation, the feeling that I was out of place. I twirled my toes in my sandals and looked at the patent leather shoes and razor-sharp creases around me. Fifty years ago Kini Maillart and Peter Fleming had crossed Tartary from Beijing to Srinigar to find themselves described as "junglies", separated from the Raj by their travels, contaminated by Asia. I felt a little jungly. Perhaps this was a separation of time, perhaps social class, possibly merely the distance between states of health. Peering dimly through the flu it was difficult to tell.

A pale woman in a beautiful pale dress said, "Have you been to Everest before?" I didn't think I was going to Everest this time, but didn't have time to explain. If I couldn't find a seat I was going to fall over. A dinner jacket bumped into my elbow, tipping liquid onto the floor. I heard myself mumbling apologies and turned to face a man in a dark collarless suit and white brimless hat, who introduced himself as an ex-ambassador to Sikkim. "So you are one of the climbers? You know, my son was a climber." At one end of the room a lectern had been set up. Rows of tubular seats had been arranged before it. Two red jackets were erecting a projection screen. Dark wood-panelling ran round the room like an elaborate and oversized skirting-board. It was, as Stephen said, all rather grand.

"Victor, please come this way, I have someone I would like you to meet." At last, rescue. Muslim led me by the arm. "You are looking ill. I will find you a seat. The man you were talking to has a very sad story. His son fell into a crevasse last summer and died, no one was able to pull him out . . . Here we are, you may sit here."

Chris and Stephen were in conversation with the Canadian consul, a tall woman in vivid green, and "S.P.". Harish and Monesh appeared to be busy arranging and rearranging the lectern and high table. The ex-ambassador, I realised, was wearing the uniform of the Congress Party and I wondered briefly if any Shiv Sena supporters were here. Renshaw and Sustad were skulking in a corner looking like a pair of schoolboys. The waiters were clearing the buffet at the back of the hall. Soon Chris was at the stand delivering his address.

The theme of the lecture was leadership. Chris ran through the Everest South-West Face expedition, showing lists of stores and equipment, the planning at every stage, how he had used critical path analysis to plan the expedition activities. "In fact this was probably the first expedition to use a computer to plan it!" he said proudly. There was one particularly impressive slide charting the progress of the expedition against previous attempts on the South-West Face. Then Chris talked about leadership techniques, especially winning the confidence of the team, for in mountaineering leadership is by consent, and how this attitude to leadership has lessons for management. At all times Chris emphasised the concept of leadership by persuasion and consent. Gradually the expedition story became a parable for management. The talk was impressive, and forced me to consider what managers might make of my own feeble efforts at mounting expeditions.

I had once been asked for the ideology behind alpine-style ascents, and I remembered that I had replied that I for one had no theoretical basis for climbing lightweight, it was just that I was far too incompetent to deal with anything bigger than a two-man ascent. I had no idea how to fix ropes, and would doubtless make an utter horlicks of camp stocking, and that it was bad enough trying to agree on food for two, the thought of trying to get agreement for a dozen was beyond the scope of imagination.

Yet here the formulae were simply laid out. I forgot I was ill, and listened with rapt attention while Sustad, two seats to my left, began to snore gently. Afterwards I saw Chris confronted by a general, or perhaps a brigadier, who said, "Yes, your ideas on leadership by consent are very interesting, but you forgot to mention discipline, surely this is the most important aspect of leadership of all!" Chris was speechless for a moment. A rare moment indeed.

After the sitting ovation, which went on for at least five minutes, I remained seated with my eyes shut, trying to meditate. It was India after all. But it was no good; either I was too ill, or simply not sufficiently mystical. Again Muslim came to my rescue, but while he searched for a waiter to bring me another drink, a reporter from the *Times of India* sat beside me and began to ask questions about the expedition, the sort of questions reporters all over the world seem to ask. Why do you do it, how did you start, and what is it like climbing with famous people like Chris Bonington. I was not up to it. My feverish brain could find no sensible answers to anything she asked. And I was still confused about the Shiv Sena transport strike that was meant to have brought Bombay to a standstill by sitting down in front of trains and being, as the paper had put it, "mildly lathi charged" for their pains. The reporter explained that was the day before. How surreal. I seemed to have missed a day.

Sometimes when you leave a cinema you are surprised by the light. You have just left the heroine in the clutches of the hero, under that starlit sky. You stand on the steps blinking as taxis hoot and pedestrians push past each other hurrying to the tube with no idea of what you have just emerged from. It is astonishing, in fact, that the day, the world even, is in full swing; and you have to re-adjust an interior clock which placed you in the dark night of dreams and fantasy. So I stood blinking on the steps of the Patkar Hall. Outside in Bombay was real life, hot, damp and very animal.

Muslim took me back to the Club in a motorcycle rickshaw. I have this memory of the rickety machine coughing and spluttering, the driver kicking the engine with his heel, like a recalcitrant steed, and angrily shouting while racing the other chariot drivers.

"Looks like he is going into battle," I shouted over the din of the Bombay rush hour as we lurched into yet another pothole.

"Of course!" said Muslim. "The taxi drivers here are Shatryas."

"What?"

"Shatryas, it is a martial caste. They are always at war. That is why the Bombay taxi drivers drive like lunatics; it is their caste."

The next day I felt better and went to the warehouse where Dick and Steve wrestled with our loads. Near by was a small temple, constructed of whitewashed bricks and arches which looked like a giant's bite marks in a monstrously large slice of bread. An old woman squatted by the door keeping the discarded shoes and sandals in neat rows, and expertly spitting squirts of red betel juice through the railings. A small girl and her brother sat in the shade holding hands. Under the entrance porch a business man bowed and knelt before a tiny altar on which he was arranging sugar cubes and rice grains. After he left I walked over to see the shapes he had made on the altar. There were two. One was a crescent, a curved dune of rice the span of a man's hand. The other had the sugar cube at its centre, and four wings of rice flowing anti-clockwise from it, the swastika. Above the offering a white stone figure sat lotus-legged, with comfortable pot belly, outspread arms garlanded with red and yellow flowers and the knowing head of an elephant. Steve and Dick finished sewing the barrels and boxes into hessian sacks for the railway journey and we left for Carmichael Road where Harish's wife, Geeta, was preparing a last supper.

"This is Ganesh," Geeta said, as she hung the silver medallion round my neck. "He is the god of new enterprises." It was the elephant god. Geeta knelt before the little family altar, from where the perfume of the incense sticks drifted in veils through Harish's study and out onto the balcony overlooking Bombay.

From Carmichael Road the townscape drops away to the Victorian Gothic library and the dome of the Victoria station. Above them the heavy grey skies, clouds pregnant with rain, were waiting for the monsoon.

"I have given a Ganesh to each member of the expedition." The silk sari swept the floor as she stood up from her prayer. "You must have some puris, come."

The Kapadia flat had one large room set out with a dining table in its centre. Tiny hollow puris, chutneys, fillings of delicately spiced mung beans, chick peas, yoghurt and a thin brown sauce flavoured with coriander, cummin, ginger and other spices I could not readily identify, decorated the table. The others were already there.

"Ah, I see you've got your Ganesh," said Stephen. His medal looked different to mine.

"Is that not a Ganesh?" I asked.

"No, it is, but Geeta gave me this one for Everest. I am sending the new one to Oliver. He'll probably swallow it." Oliver was Stephen's baby son.

"Is that wise? I mean, if Ganesh is meant to be for new projects, shouldn't you keep the new one?" But Stephen's attention had been diverted. Harish was demonstrating a new combination of fillings for the puris.

The entire team, with the exception of Graham, who was joining us in Delhi, was gathered here, some clutching baby puris and others beginning on the mangoes. Harish's team, Vijay Kothari, a velvet manufacturer, little Monesh Devjani, a merchant banker, worried about the current crisis in the Bombay stock exchange, Bhupesh Ashar, a sales executive, and Muslim Contractor who was in his family's ink manufacturing business, spilled not a drop, while the Westerners splashed the spices and squashy mangoes on themselves and the table. I noted that we were a team of Gudjeratis and Maharatis, an American, a Scot, a token Welshman from Yorkshire, and a couple of English, including me. Or to look at it another way, three Hindus of various castes, a Jain, a Muslim, a Lutheran, an atheist Catholic, and a few agnostic Protestants two of whom were vegetarians. I fingered the strange medallion that was to hang round my neck during the following weeks, bringing Hindu blessings and intercessions with the deities.

Chapter Sixteen

Steaming to Madkot

Any train journey in India is a unique experience, travelling not only in space but in time, on railways that are a product of the Raj, and have remained largely unchanged, except in one remarkable respect, and perhaps this too owes something to an imperial penchant for organisation. This is the computerisation of the booking system. You know where you will sit, in which carriage, on what train, the moment you put your money down. On the day, lists of passengers and bookings are displayed before the platforms. The system is efficient, and it covers all India. Take note, British Rail. Yet even this metaphor for progress, borrowed from aviation, is subverted with bribery and favours. It is a very Indian solution to the straitjacket of systems ideology. So when we returned, at the end of the expedition, too late to take up our places which had been booked on the Rajasthan Express three months in advance, all was not lost. A hundred rupees here, fifty there, a family contact with the management, and the computer was persuaded that 202 plus 6 equals 202.

There are several classes of travel, from first-class sleeper to third-class seats. We travelled AC (air conditioned). The trains are drawn by steam engines like shire horses, settling down at the buffers with powerful sighs and clouds of steam rising into the iron vaults. Bombay Central station, built by contractors from Yorkshire and the Black Country, looks a little like the glass and cast-iron sheds of St Pancras and King's Cross, probably contemporary and no doubt influenced by the Paxton's Crystal Palace at the 1851 Great Exhibition, as were the Russians who modelled their station architecture on Vauxhall Gardens, and to this day call their stations *voksals*.

Behind the sighing steam engine, the sides of the carriages were dusty with travel. A line of square portholes were punched out of the flat sheet steel. The third-class carriages had no glass in the windows, only mild steel reinforcing bars welded across the opening. Scrawny fingers gripped the bars, dark brown faces grimaced behind. It was an extraordinary sight, sheets of steel, decorated with television screen-size holes, each with its own collection of masks.

Everyone has this image of the Pukka Englishman in Asia, dressed in old-fashioned sporting gear, the shorts not quite meeting the calf stockings. Venables, standing pink-faced beside me, matched the image exactly. I pointed to the faces in the carriage.

"Bit like that Ezra Pound haiku, isn't it?"

"What one?"

"You know, it goes:
>   'In a station of the Metro
>   The apparition of these faces in the crowd;
>   Petals on a wet, black bough.' "

And I pointed at the frowning faces. But Venables was no longer listening. That woman reporter from the *Times of India* wanted a last photograph of Stephen and Chris boarding the train.

The AC coaches were painted a rust red colour to match the dust, and had dark glass in the square, permanently shut windows. We peered out through the glass darkly as Bombay fell away, then the parched red plains rolled past. Out there the villagers were starving while the city consumed their water. Harish said they were waiting for the monsoon, when the villages would grow their one crop of rice, then abandon the fields to the red dust again. The attendant brought dinky little thermos flasks of tea. Later he would bring curried chicken and parathas and tiny spiced shish kebabs, and later still samosas and biscuits and more tea. The plains flooded past our window. We kicked off our shoes and let our feet breathe the cool conditioned air. The Stephens read and hibernated. Dick produced a small notepad and soft pencil. Harish went back to his team in the next compartment and Chris and I had our first chess game of the expedition. It was wonderful, almost a holiday within a holiday.

We rolled into Delhi sipping morning tea from the dinky thermoses. There were more lectures from Stephen and Chris, who was described in glowing terms to the packed audience. "He is a very strong climber and continues to do so, which is a very rarity to do so for long and stay safe." I am not poking fun at this peculiarly Indian sentence, I am intrigued by the different dialect. Sometimes it is straight out of the past, you'd recognise your grandparents using the same phrases. And yet these Indian English constructions often convey a different sense and meaning to what we automatically translate them into. And we are in danger of missing this, which is a pity.

After the lectures there was an outdoor reception in the gardens of the Hotel Kaneshka. It was here that we met our Liaison Officer, Wing Commander Anil Srivastava.

"You may call me Anil, or Winko. That is what they call me in the Air Force."

Winko had brought with him a rare and prized treasure, a military map of the Panch Chuli area. Venables and I had seen one of these during the Rimo Expedition in 1985. They were drawn to the same standard as old one-inch OS sheets, but the existence of these maps was always officially denied. The general public had to make do with sketches at one to quarter-million scale. A visit to the India Office library earlier in the year showed that, though all British India had been surveyed at the one-inch scale, military paranoia (probably inherited from the British) had prevented the general publication of maps of the Himalayan region. Yet it is difficult to imagine a serious enemy of India without access to the most detailed satellite imagery, should they want it.

Graham Little had just completed our party. He had flown to Delhi from Edinburgh where he works for the Ordnance Survey, and was so intrigued by the map, he persuaded Winko to lend it for a while, provided we made no copies, or not in colour anyway.

Luxurious AC travel had now come to an end and we proceeded from Delhi by bus over the northern plains to Ranikhet, a hill station at 1500 metres, where roses and chestnut trees grew among pines, and then down to the thick hot air of the lower Himalayan valleys, crowded with rice fields and dense forest. Sometimes we recognised an acacia, or a rooty banyan. Mostly we tried to sleep, because the bus was horrible. The seats were too close to stretch the legs, the metal tubing poking through the backs hit us like sticks with each bump. And there were a lot of those. Attempts at reading produced nausea. Talk was only possible with the person next to you and then at full volume. The hot air blew through the open windows like a blast furnace. Sweat ran down the back of the plastic-covered seats and soaked the waist band of the shorts. I remember that Venables enlivened things at one chai stop with vivid descriptions of bivouacking with Dave Wilkinson, and Dave's unique solution to the oldest problem of mountaineering, how to defecate while bivouacking in a storm, without leaving the tent. It was not a pleasant tale, but one we would remember later to good effect.

At Baidrinaj, another chai stop, there was the most beautiful, serene and ancient temple decaying at the edges. Well vibrated by the bus, we staggered down the path to admire. Something familiar about the detail carved in the stone tiles and moulding kept evading me.

Steve said, "Looks like timber details."

Of course! The monks or whoever had constructed this building had evidently used timber construction methods. Perhaps they, like the Greeks, had evolved their stone temples from timber barns. Perhaps, like the Victorians when confronted with new materials like cast iron, had simply not adjusted their design to the new and unusual properties. In any case, the Baidrinaj temple looks, in part at least, like a stone model of a wooden building.

At last, bruised and shaken, we noticed that the bus had come to a standstill. It was eight o'clock, and darkening fast. Anil a.k.a. Winko had taken off his shirt and was tinkering with the engine. The Westerners all wanted to know what was wrong, and how long it would be before we got moving again, though Harish took an Indian view, and settled down for the duration. Sustad did too, pointing out that it was much more comfortable now the bus was still. After an hour it became clear that the engine was properly broken, and Dick wondered if we might not walk to the next stop. It was dark outside, and no doubt wild animals had begun to prowl. No one was very keen, but Dick persisted. He asked Winko to ask the driver how far it was. The driver motioned to a grey flat-topped building beside us. Winko looked confused and asked the man again, then explained, slowly, so that we could understand.

"This is the rest house." He pointed at the building at the back of which we had broken down. "But the parking is in the front of the rest house. So he must mend the bus first."

We stared in disbelief at the back of the rest house. I suppose the driver had not thought to tell us, because nobody had bothered to ask him.

This was Munsiary. Dawn the next day brought the entire team out onto the verandah. Rising through the mist was the faint but distinct outline of the main peak, Panch Chuli II. White on white, filmy with mist. Harish said, "When the cloud clears we shall be able to see the whole Panch Chuli group totally." The rest of the day was spent slitting open the gunny sacks and repacking the loads. Above the rest house the acacia forest took over from the road edge. But below, a neat stone-flagged path found its way through the terraced fields and, between furious bouts of repacking, we'd wander down to the tiny market-place. Brown shacks made a square around the central area, which was mostly dark mud of indeterminate but definitely suspicious origin. A pair of ugly mongrels had taken it upon themselves to guard the market against any possible customers. The main or high alley led down from the square (actually, Munsiary is a one-alley town), small shacks on either side traded in the sort of merchandise you always seem to find in the extreme backwaters of the Himalaya, cheap soap, cloths and simple tailoring, various root vegetables, mangoes and soft bananas, guavas, sometimes fresh, often overripe, weeping and odoriferous.

Harish found a chai house restaurant that fed all of us with boiled rice, dhal thinly cooked with onion and garlic, and soft sabjee (this time the vegetable was a turnip curry). Graham pushed his plate away after a few mouthfuls and tactfully declared himself strangely unhungry. Sustad gobbled up all his and took Graham's too. Dick, Chris and I tucked into the hot chapatis with real enjoyment. Fresh bread in any language is delicious.

Harish said he was impressed with this Pukka English team (Welsh, Scots and American are apparently sub-species of English to him) all eating the Indian food without complaint. The Chong Kumdan team had been quite different. They had, according to Harish, preferred starvation to dhal and rice. Sustad mumbled something about only ever eating out at Indians in London anyway, but I couldn't hear him properly between the eager slurps of dhal.

Twenty-two kilometres across the other side of the valley the terminal settlement, Madkot, existed in parochial isolation from the world. It took the bus two hours to plough there through the pre-monsoon mud. Madkot is an extraordinarily appropriate-sounding name. It was a town of blank looks. Not even a shake of the head in response to a question. All of us, Westerners and Indians alike, got the same blank response. Perhaps Madkot was a town of xenophobes, perhaps it was the result of generations of inbreeding, but the look in their eyes was a look that indicated utter alienation. Yet this was the place where we would have to hire porters.

Bhupesh, Monesh and Harish had disappeared to search for some, a decidedly bleak prospect. After several hours they were seen approaching, followed by what looked like a crowd of ragged beggars. An argument broke out among the crowd.

But we had our own mini-crisis. Chris couldn't find his wallet, hadn't seen it since we boarded the bus at Delhi two days ago.

"You know, it's very worrying; I definitely put it in the top flap of the rucksack."

Sustad thought it would turn up eventually, providing we stopped looking for it. No one was prepared to voice the unthinkable, that it had been stolen.

Meanwhile the ragged army's argument had escalated into a small-scale riot. Monesh, Bhupesh and Harish retreated quickly to join us. Bhupesh breathlessly explained:

"These people are all crooks. The contractor agreed the walk-up in three days. The return is half-rate. Four and a half rounded up equals five days. But the contractor is offering the boys four days only, and he is keeping the remainder of the sum."

"The main worry is the credit cards," said Chris, looking through his camera case for the fugitive wallet.

"Have you looked in the map pocket?" asked Dick helpfully.

"This sack doesn't have one, does it? Oh, it does!" Chris found yet another zip. "But I couldn't have put the wallet in there if I didn't even know about it." He unzipped the new pocket and something small and black fell out. "Oh, my wallet!"

But Chris was spared the embarrassment. The porters had quite suddenly decided to end their contractual dispute and started picking loads for the trek into the jungly valleys.

Chapter Seventeen

Under the Dribbling Snout

Over the next three days our path dwindled in size as we left behind first the town of Madkot, then villages, the last one being called Ringo, slowly climbing across terraced slopes which became increasingly uncultivated, till we found ourselves 300 metres above the river, which flowed like molten silver in the green V below us.

Across the gorge, whitewashed farmhouses caught the evening sun, glowing in a nest of tiger stripes created by the terraced fields, yellow with corn, separated by grey-green hedged walls.

The path left the fields and crossed intermittent clearings before plunging into the unrelieved green-canopied forest. We had split into walking groups, and I found myself with Muslim, who gestured at the corridor of leaves.

"This is classic *Jungle Book* jungle."

"Yes," I said. "This is the real thing, primary montane forest. Best enjoy it while it is still around!"

Something dark and small flitted between the trees, and made a "whoop! whoop!" sound. Low fleshy undergrowth betrayed the muddy passage of a forest stream. We stopped to fill our water-bottles. Freed from the rustle of our clothes and the monotonous hammer of our steps, the ears could now listen to the forest. A high warbling from the ground ivy was answered from the canopy above us. There was a screaming peacock-like call, buzzings and chirpings.

Camp that night was under a stand of huge deodars. Sixty metres above us the red trunks fanned out in branches of needles. We cooked on the cedar-scented cones. Drifting smoke, mist glimpsed between the giant trunks, showed where the porters had settled down for the night, huddled in blankets round the small fires, sipping from broken enamel cups, and nibbling fresh chapatis.

Inside his tent Chris was swearing at himself.

"Bonington, you *nana*! You *silly* idiot!"

"What is the problem, Chris, can we help?" asked Muslim, looking worried.

"Well, only if you promise not to tell anyone."

"OK, Chris, I promise."

"It's that zoom camera Olympus sent me. I haven't seen it since Ringo. I took some shots of the farms across the valley, and I think I must have put the camera down on a rock."

Muslim brought in a large kitbag marked CB and stuffed full with photographic equipment, which Chris poked about inside.

"No, not here . . . I can't get worked up about these damned electronic gadgets. I would have walked back to Ringo for the OM4. But not for this." Chris took another despairing look into the kitbag and pulled out a black object in an Ever Ready case.

"Oh. It's here," he said, then looked Muslim and me straight in the face. "Remember, you promised not to tell anyone." But it was too late, I had already summoned Sustad.

That night, as on every night of the walk-in, the thunder stormed round the forest. Branched lightning silhouetted the tree-fringed hills above the valley. Venables set up his tripod and Nikon. He spent so much of his time writing his diary or taking photographs, it was frightening. I had no idea what he was writing about us, and in order to get my retaliation in first began to list in my diary all his obvious faults. Like being conscientious, and taking too many photographs. The thunder brought a tattoo of rain on the tent, and deep peaceful sleep. There can be no sound in the world more comforting when you are safely under canvas in your soft, dry sleeping bag.

The path became even less distinct. The trees changed from conifer to deciduous; rhododendron, maple and chestnut dominated the hillside. The forest path led us past a man-made clearing where two foresters were cutting up a red-fleshed tree none of us had seen before with a three-metre log saw. An end of the trunk was supported above the ground, and one man stood on top of the trunk, his assistant on the ground.

Sustad explained. "That's good. Instead of digging a sawpit they have stuck the trunk up in the air. The man on top is topdog, he just pulls the saw blade up again, doesn't do any of the cutting strokes. It's the one underneath who does all the work."

"What's he called?"

"He is the underdog."

"Is that where the name comes from?"

"Yeah, they used to make the apprentices be underdog for ten years before they got to be on top. It's real dirty. You get all that sawdust in your face."

Dick couldn't resist trying it himself. He lasted about five minutes as underdog.

In the afternoon the path, which had now become more of an animal track, led to a clear stream which tumbled over grey boulders. A thin fog collected in banks under the trees. The edges of the water lapped against red-stained mud.

"This is Balati," said Muslim. "The water is hot here." On the map the place was marked Hot Spring, Balati Gadhera. I have a sequence of slides of a lobster-red Christian Bonington, head, knees and book above the steaming water. In the first slide he is deeply entranced, reading. But what is the book? Maybe a guide to Himalayan flora? A closer shot reveals the embossed cover of an airport book. It is Jilly Cooper's *Riders*. The next slide shows Chris looking up at the camera, surprised and perhaps a little embarrassed.

"I have to finish this before getting down to my diary," Chris explained, trying to hide the cover.

The track kept disappearing under the dense foliage; sometimes it split into equally indistinct branches, slipping under fallen trunks, or through the long grasping arms of a rhododendron. The path had not been made for humans. Thickets of bamboo punctuated the forest floor, and slowly we became aware of a growing rumble. The way now lay close to the Balati torrent. Dark rich leaf compost gave way to a sandier stone-filled soil, and the track climbed up and down features that may have been the remains of moraines. Smaller trees and shrubs let in more light. It was ideal for flowering plants. The eye was constantly halted by tiny explosions of colour.

"*Aha!* Lithospermum!" It was Venables, of course. Two steps further on he stopped again. White knobbly knees, flapping jungle shorts. Garlanded with cameras.

"*Aha!* Piptanthus nepalensis laburnifolius! . . . I promise you. We have one in our garden and I promised Rosie to bring back photographs of them in flower. We can't get ours to flower, because of the frost."

"Why not?" I asked. "It must freeze here too." But he had bounded on to another tussock.

After two days the path burst out of the forests; it had taken us above the tree-line. The way now lay up the boulder-strewn edge of the Balati torrent. The map, drawn in 1962, showed the snout of the Uttari Balati Glacier and the snout of the Dakhini Balati Glacier joining in a Y shape at about 3000 metres. But the global warming of the last decade has produced glacial retreats throughout the northern hemisphere. The Dakhini Balati must have tumbled into the Balati Gadhera with an impressively large icefall. For now the snout was an enormous ice wedge squeezing out through a high gap in the moraine wall. We looked up at the wedge, 300 metres above us. Our goal, the snout of the Uttari Balati, had also been moved.

Retreating at the rate of 30 metres or so a year, the glacier was now two-thirds of a mile upstream of its 1962 location. It terminated in a monstrously large slag-heap, dribbling stones and boulders, as if in the grip of some ridiculous asthmatic allergy. Our Base was under that dribbling snout.

It was exciting to arrive at our new home. The team busied themselves setting up the tents. Muslim, Vijay and Monesh sorted out the stores. Bhupesh paid off the porters with Winko's assistance. Sustad and Dick, the woodworkers, helped erect the kitchen tarpaulin with bits of tree scavenged from the nearby woods. Venables was sorting out his cameras and writing his diary, while I took the trenching spade to a soft spot downwind of the camp to exercise my architectural skills excavating latrines.

Chris, Harish and Graham settled down to a long conference in Chris's enormous Hypernova tent. Tea and biscuits were brought at regular intervals. Now was the time to see how the varied aspirations of the group would fit together.

It could be seen from Winko's map that the Uttari Balati Glacier climbed up from our Base at 3200 metres over six or seven kilometres through a deep but wide gorge. At 4800 metres this opened out into a six-kilometre-wide basin surrounded by a ring of 6000-metre peaks. Panch Chuli II (6904m), the highest peak of the group and the primary objective of the trip, had been first climbed in 1973 by the Indo-Tibetan Border Police, following a route pioneered by Heinrich Harrer in 1951. Most of the other surrounding peaks had not been climbed, though Rajrambha had been claimed from another valley system.

Previous expedition reports indicated three major icefalls which could all be turned by excursions on the right bank. Chris, Graham and Harish pored over the map, made calculations for porter-loads,

tried to establish how long it would take to acclimatise while trans-
porting loads from 3200 to 4800 metres, and then on to 6000 metres
where another plateau would form a kicking-off point for Panch
Chuli II.

On the mountain we were to split up into three teams, working from
the same Advanced Base Camp. Harish's team would attempt Panch
Chuli II via the South-West Ridge, the line of the first ascent. The
1973 ascent had involved fixing almost the entire route with fixed rope
by a very large team. Harish was going to try a lightweight ascent.
This was the "A" team. Chris and Graham, the "B" team, would
try a new route on the West Ridge of the same mountain. Dick, the
Stephens and I were going to kick off with one of the 6000-metre
peaks, we weren't sure which, then perhaps look at Panch Chuli II,
the "C" team.

This was a complicated set of objectives to fit into the short time
we had available. But expedition programming was the thing Chris
was particularly good at. This was his Grande Forte. He gleefully
produced his secret weapon, the Macintosh. He had just acquired
the brand new notebook computer, complete with solar cells and
batteries. And here was a task just made for the machine.

Chris made a drawing showing Base Camp, the first icefall, an
intermediate camp, two more icefalls, an Advance Base at 4800 metres,
then the route diverging, one branch to the "C" team objective in the
direction of Rajrambha, with several bivouacs, and one branch to
Camp 1 at 6000 metres and on to Panch II. The diagram was like
a board game. You had to establish x number of climbers on each
set of summits, which required y loads of provisions at z camps. In
fact this board game was not far short of Chris's favourite computer
pastime, Strategic Conquest, which he kept on the Macintosh. Over
the course of the expedition I just about held my own with the chess,
but was overrun in the Strategic Conquest series every single time.

Chris had visualised the climbers spending a few days at each
level, then descending to base for R & R (rest and recuperation,
military term, I am told). This would provide the right level of
fitness and acclimatisation for the summit push. Chris and Harish
between them established tentative dates for each camp, the number
of loads required in good weather, and a contingency for the predicted
bad weather, the amount of food needed at Base for the returning
climbers and so on. After a few hours the pieces all fell into place,
or so it had seemed.

There was only one thing that was rather puzzling. The Indians had brought three tents, exactly enough for themselves for only one camp at a time. Evidently they had planned to cut off their retreat by moving up the tents at the same time as the loads, cook, kitchen tent and all, but they had not mentioned this before the Great Conference. I guessed that Harish was a little bit in awe of Chris's reputation, and tended to agree to the great man's proposals without mentioning his own previous plans. Meanwhile Chris, deeply considerate and democratic human being that he is, was trying to find out what it was the Indians really wanted to do. Neither Chris nor Harish wanted to give offence to the other, and the pair seemed to circle each other.

There are times when democracy can be a disadvantage. There is an often-recounted and many-versioned story of the mercurial Doug Scott on K2. All versions end with Doug disagreeing with the others, who suggest that the matter be put to the vote. "You know, youth," replied Doug, "democracy is a bit of a failure if you end up having to vote on it." Quite so, Doug. The resolution to the tent shortage was cosy. We shared the tents we had between us.

After the Great Conference, our cook, who looked like Lee Van Cleef but called himself Revatram, produced kedgeree and pumpkin, followed by endless pots of chai. We had had a long day, Muslim's eyelids could hardly hold themselves up. Venables and Dick retired to write diaries and draw sketches. Sustad had just started a new book, and Chris and Graham settled down to a long chess duel.

It was dark, and the tents glowed like night-lights, one by one slipping back into the night. A cool breeze wafted down from the unseen bulk of the Dribbling Snout. Someone in Bhupesh's tent began to snore gently. This calm and restful scene was suddenly and rudely disturbed.

"Oh, you bleeding *idiot*! . . . you've *blown* it!" The chess was seemingly not going Chris's way, for Graham could be heard chuckling in a most unsympathetic manner.

Much later, when all the tents bar one were dark, and the symphony of snoring ebbed and flowed in gentle crescendo and diminuendo, there was another outburst from the lone lit tent.

"*Haha!* . . . you lose your queen too!" But no one else was awake to hear it.

Chapter Eighteen

Rajrambha

Harish enjoyed his food, and as form follows function, so his shape was pleasantly rounded. Especially round the middle. He kept his hair short; perhaps it was thinning slightly. There were beads of perspiration on his brow from the sheer effort of the devouring. The sharp eyes filled with concentration as the next course arrived.

"Ha, Tony Bhai!" (which is how he always called me). "How do you like this bhel?"

"Mmmm, mmmm, mmmm." My mouth was stuffed full of the savoury ricicles and chutney. So I nodded.

A tall pole held up the centre of the red kitchen tarpaulin, a large boulder, a bit of dry-stone walling and ski sticks supported the edges. The diurnal thunderstorm was pouring rain over the whole edifice, and pools of water collected in the folds of the tents like enormous breasts. All previous expedition reports had commented on the endemic bad weather in the region. It had to be admitted, it was wet here. Venables, who had taken to wearing a felt Homburg, stood up to empty the water from one of the breasts, while Harish finished with his story.

He told us how in Hindu mythology guardian fairies protect the Devas from the interfering mortals. Rajrambha was the most beautiful of the guardian fairies. The 6537-metre mountain which takes this name is correspondingly the most beautiful of the western outliers to the Panch Chuli, protecting the place of the last meal of the Pandavas. Panch is five, Chuli, cooking pot, symbolising the five elements to which the human body returns after death. It's all in that great Sanskrit epic, the *Mahabarata*. As we worked on the tortuous Uttari Balati Glacier, the view was dominated by

Rajrambha, every bit as beautiful to our eyes as the legend has suggested.

There were a couple of dead ends, of course. There always are. Graham and Chris found a neat way round the first icefall, by an easy gully to a shrubby knoll which overlooked the glacier. There we established a temporary camp on the ice, and ferried loads while looking for a route past the next obstacle.

The second icefall was initially turned on the left bank by an excursion through unstable séracs and up a stone shoot. This was far too dangerous for Harish's Manali men to follow and Dick recognised this when he reached the top, but he had also noticed a safer line on the right bank. So the four of us, Dick, the Stephens and I, decided to go down the Renshaw Route. Dick's route climbed up from the glacier and followed a rocky diagonal ledge to a saddle, from which a long but easy snow-filled couloir led down, back to the Intermediate camp. There was one tricky step, a line of shattered shale overhung the diagonal ledge, and barred entrance to the groove above. Dick went up first, pulling some loose bricks out, which bounced down the scree below us to the glacier. Venables followed him but stopped in the middle of the hard move. "*Aha*, a macrophylla! It's beautiful . . ." But he was holding on with both hands and couldn't reach his camera. Sustad started to berate him. "Stephen! We're waiting . . ." but I held Sustad's arm and said:

"Let him, after all it's him that's about to fall off, not us."

Coming down from the saddle we noticed Harish's team had already started to climb what was later called the Indian Couloir.

We lunched on the glacier, by a clear surface stream. Venables produced a salad from his rucksack. He'd found wild garlic leaves, and something that tasted like chicory, but looked like acanthus. He tossed the ingredients in mayonnaise and threw in a tin of smoked mussels.

It took nine days to reach and establish Advance Base Camp and all that time the sight of Rajrambha transfixed us. On 29 May, Harish arrived at the camp at the same time as a particularly evil-looking set of black cumulus clouds. He brought the post. Three letters for Monesh. Nothing else. We'd been looking forward to news from home. Things were going on that we could never have guessed: a Government minister had been caught *in flagrante delicto*, the Royal family had begun to auto-destruct and, sadly, Wanda Rutkiewicz had disappeared on Kangchengjunga. But at the time this was all unknown to us.

"Have you noticed," said Sustad, who was beginning his scare-crow impersonation, "that whenever Harish arrives the weather seems to get worse?"

"Don't worry, Stephen Bhai. We are in for a change of weather. The Hindu calendar predicts a silver lining for the last day of the month."

Chris agreed. "Looks like the weather pattern has changed. So Graham and I are going to set off this afternoon. We'll bivi under that wall." He pointed to the 1000-metre wall under Nagalaphu. They expected to spend two days traversing that mountain.

The gusts grew stronger throughout the night, till the tents were buckling under the strain, flysheets were flapping furiously, flashes of lightning lit up the interiors, hailstones sounded like someone pouring bucketsful of ballbearings into a tin dustbin. "This is the worst mountain storm I've been in since Makalu," Sustad said. We huddled round our stove which was burning badly and giving us both ferocious headaches. I clutched my Ganesh medal, and wondered if Chris was wearing his.

Dick was worried about Chris and Graham, somewhere on the far side of the basin, surrounded by avalanche slopes. When dawn came, we couldn't make out any tracks where the pair should have been. The wind abated with the growing light. Chris and Graham's tent, a Supernova they had left behind at ABC, had disappeared, blown away by the tempest. Later that morning Bhupesh found it in the middle of the glacier, cameras and film mixed with porridge, cheese and sweets.

Sustad had also had a terrible night. He had found an empty "5 Pints" bottle which he used as a pee bottle. It was too horrible to go outside. But it was only when he had filled the bottle that he noticed the hole. The pee bottle itself was now peeing onto his tent floor.

Dick waited till late morning, then filled a sack with first-aid things and a spare sleeping bag. Carrying the rope I prepared to follow him. It often happens like this; no sooner had we geared ourselves up than the sun peeped out from the clouds, and there in the far distance, helmets glinting in the light, miles from Nagalaphu, on completely the wrong side of the glacier, emerged Chris and Graham. I touched my Ganesh appreciatively.

"We made the most colossal balls-up," Chris was slurping tea, rosy cheeks emerging from the rustic beard so badly in need of a hedge-trimmer. "We really thought we were much further up the glacier than we were."

"Yes, it is really difficult to gauge your distance in bad weather," added Graham, who knows something about wandering about in foul weather. Working for the Ordnance Survey he lost his compass long ago, and since that time has wandered about the Scottish mountains without one. His understanding of the three-dimensional translation of maps and his map memory were such that, in twenty years, he only once tried to descend the wrong gully on Ben Nevis. In a white-out he'd got as far as lowering his legs over the cornice of Comb Gully, before submitting to the sixth sense and climbing back onto the plateau.

"No, no, what we really did," Chris had evidently been struck by a new thought, "what we really did was to change our plans in view of the conditions; we were exploring the new route to Panch II." There was polite laughter all round, Monesh wagging his head, Sustad guffawing.

After the Night of the Great Storm, Chris and Graham said they would go down to Base, and we thought we'd join them. But first the four of us decided to climb a training peak of about 6000 metres, an elegant but unnamed pyramid of snow and ice above the ABC. Venables woke up at 3.00 a.m. shouting across the tents that he had lost his headtorch. We had taken separate tents as usual. After four years of bivouacking Sustad and I still didn't share tents, given the choice. I still snore, and he sleep-talks more than ever.

"Has anyone seen my torch?"

"When did you see it last?" said Sustad sleepily, attempting to apply logic before dawn.

"Outside the tent, on my ice axe." We heard the ice-crusted zip slice open the front of the tent. "Oh, it's still there!"

I began to wonder if Stephen had caught this strange new symptom from Chris, or was it perhaps a permanent sign, a stigma attached to all who had ascended Everest?

It was my turn to brew. It generally is in the mornings; Sustad does the evenings. I shifted the sleeping bag round and sat the stove in a snow pocket in the porch, put on a one-litre billy, and reached for the snow under the tent flap with a plastic cup. As I wore no gloves, the snow stuck in flakes and lumps to my fingers. I rammed the cup into the growing hole under the flap and scooped up two more cups. The billy was full, it would take ten minutes to melt the three cups of snow and produce a few spoons of water. Meanwhile I could retreat back into the sleeping bag and suck the cold fingers until the warmth came back. The snow scooping would have to be repeated again and again, until the pan was full. Twenty minutes' respite deep in sleeping bag until the water boiled and tea could be made. Twenty minutes to appreciate the comfort of four inches of goose down and toasty warm toes, and consider in which order to pull on the boots. Twenty minutes in which to wish we were at home, with nothing more horrible to look forward to than the climbing wall and possibly a pint or two of beer to follow.

I was still thinking about the beer as we trudged uphill, leaving a line of knee-deep holes, towards our training peak. Being the slowest of the group, I was expected to go first. (Shows how gullible you can be under flattery. What the other three wanted was someone daft enough to break trail without complaint.) The first sign of altitude for the year. Legs turning to lead. Breathing out with each step. Stopping to breathe in. Then across the bergschrund, and unroping. Dick, Sustad and I reached a ridge after two hours on the south-facing slope. It was 7.30 and the snow was softening fast. We were at about 5800 metres, and the summit was another hour away. We conferred. That is to say we chewed a Lion bar and stared down into the valley below. Venables, hung about with cameras, was still on the slopes below us. We decided that to continue would not help our acclimatisation, and to delay the descent while the snow turned to slush, and our steps collapsed in the heat, would be boring. Sustad smirked at the word "boring". 'That's real typical English, like the way you use the word 'interesting'."

But we hadn't counted on Venables. When we turned to descend he had just reached the ridge, and was looking over the other side, at our Base Camp and the line of our walk-in along the Balati Gadhera. Turning to see us, he must have thought we were on the way down from the top, for he completely lost his temper. The language was appalling.

"*Aha,*" I said to Dick and Sustad, "the Venables Tantrum. Famous throughout London." Now he was waving his axes in the air.

"We'd better calm him down before he does himself an injury," said Dick. So we shouted down that we had not in fact been to the top. It is a strange but comforting fact that Venables Tantra always pass in minutes, and by the time we reached him, he had recovered his composure.

"Fantastic view . . . That mountain there," Venables pointed unsteadily behind him, "must be Api or Saipal . . . I just wanted some shots of you on the ridge," he added sheepishly. We were back at ABC by 10.30, wading in porridge.

For the last two weeks our landscape had been dominated by Rajrambha's South Face, which had been our original target, a wall of fluted ice ribs and rocky outcrops. But the excursion on the training peak suggested that this would consist largely of sun-soaked deep snow on steep mixed ground, and it was Dick who first suggested the integral traverse, a journey of some ten kilometres, about half of which would be over 6000 metres. A sort of giant Peuterey Ridge I suppose. For comparison, the Peuterey finishes on the summit of Mont Blanc at 4807 metres, while our ABC was just a bit higher at 4840 metres. This near-coincidence was pointed out, of course, by Graham the Cartologist.

From ABC our western skyline formed the route. There was a low col at the head of the glacier due north of us. We'd start there, then follow the skyline from right to left. We could see a mixed-entry buttress to the ridge, then a summit of about 6000 metres, Menaka (another of those fairies, of course), then a long and possibly corniced ridge, three more mixed buttresses, the last of which was undoubtedly very steep, more heavily corniced ridges, and a giant summit cornice. The descent looked deceptively straightforward. Amble down a sort of mixed buttress with bulging séracs, find a narrow col, and a final 600 metres of front pointing down to the glacier should see us walking home. Well, almost. There were a couple of cards that nature had dealt that were not in our favour.

First there was the weather. Notwithstanding the Great Storm, the diurnal stormlets here, at 4800 metres, in the Uttari Balati Plateau, were quite violent enough. Clouds with towering black anvils blossomed every day, usually by lunch time. Thunder, lightning and thrashing hailstorms followed in the afternoon. The noise on the tent was extraordinarily loud, like thousands of angry millipedes crawling over a microphone. By early night the energy driving these microcosms had been drained, and clear skies would return for another twelve hours. The second card was the sheer spiteful ferocity of the sun. By 8.00 a.m. every day the snow had softened till it was thigh deep. It did not begin to freeze again till nightfall. Our window of opportunity was therefore between the end of the storms at, say, midnight and the softening of the snow at 9.00 a.m.

There was one more thing, nature had imbued us with the propensity to underestimate almost everything. So we thought that, unacclimatised as we were, we would still be able to do the traverse inside three days. This would be a straightforward, quick and, above all, safe climb. Perhaps.

The idea was simplicity itself. One Stephen and I would take a tent and one rope, Dick and the other Stephen would do the same. Each pair would take three days' food. We'd be able to cut down on hardware, and share ropes for the abseils. We would climb quite a lot of the ridge and all the lower buttresses in the dark. We planned to stop by 8.30, perhaps 9.00 a.m. at the latest.

It was a minor nuisance that when either Dick or I called Steve, the answer came back in stereo, but a solution was at hand. While packing for the traverse, Harish or Muslim, I don't remember which, noticed that Venables was wearing his felt Homburg over the hood of his jacket, and bore an uncanny resemblance to Freddy Kruger. Of course Stephen had never heard of *Nightmare on Elm Street* and looked utterly bemused when Harish said, "So is it Nightmare on Balati tonight, Stephen Bhai?"

Such is the infantile mentality of the Himalayan climber that within minutes we all were calling Venables Freddy, just to enjoy his uncomprehending and slightly exasperated stare. That still left Sustad answering to Stephen but he's the Lutheran mentioned earlier, so sometimes we called for the American, at other times we asked for the Lutheran, and just occasionally, when deeply muddled, hung around with slings and nuts and pegs, unable to get things right, we might have forgotten ourselves so far as to use his real name.

We set off during the night of 1 June, Freddy and the Lutheran stomping across the expanse of glacier to the start of the climb, preceded by small pools of torchlight. Soon Dick would take over, leaving me plodding asthmatically in their steps. Warnings floated out of the dark, "Slot here!" or "Watch the rope a second!". The back marker (me) would take in a few coils and brace himself for the shock which never came. We always took the utmost care with crevasses. That's how you grow old as a climber.

It was so still that the air, though well below freezing, felt warm. Later there was a slight breeze, enough to strip the layer of warmed air from the body. That's normal, the predawn breeze seems as much a feature of mountain meteorology as the katabatic wind. The breeze died away with the growing light. We crossed the bergschrund, where we unroped, and began soloing up the easy buttresses.

There was a small but beautiful coincidence; we reached the

watershed ridge at the same moment as the thin morning sun. The view was new to us. The silver ridge unfolded above us in rolled volumes, ranks of pale ridges and peaks marched away into the Tibetan mists. We could clearly see Harrer's route to Panch Chuli II which Chris and Harish would be following. Not long afterwards the sun grew stronger and the snow softer. Soon we were panting for air under heavy rucksacks and sweltering heat, and looking for the first possible tent site.

That afternoon we lay exhausted, making desultory brews, too hot to sleep. The Lutheran said, "You know, the most difficult thing about Himalayan climbing is dealing with the extremes of temperature." He had surprised us by bringing a book. *The Good Terrorist*. We tried to get him to read us passages; he wouldn't, but did give us a one-line précis: "It's about people with cockney accents, who start speaking BBC English when they get angry." He pushed his shoulder-length hair out of his way, and tried to smooth down his beard so it would not interrupt his view of the book. Already his salopettes were stained with spilt food.

The tent poles froze solid the next morning and I broke one. Speaking gently to it in BBC English, I packed it away leaving bits of pole sticking out. For the rest of the trip my sack sported long whippy antennae. This was to become significant.

Over the next two days Freddy, the American, Dick and I travelled slowly as snails over Menaka and down to the long col before the last steep buttress. Sometimes there were delightfully steep pitches on barely frozen shale, more often we were creeping sideways on ice, covered thinly with a faithless film of powder, and trying to stay below the cornice line; at the end of each day the sun deepening the snow. Usually the climbing was brittle and insecure and needed a lot of care and some pitching.

By late morning on day four we could look back with some satisfaction on the ridge, winding like a country road above the deep shadowed valleys. We'd had a couple of exhilarating sections of very Scottish climbing, tiptoeing in crampons, fist jams, rock-overs on snow-covered rock and unbalanced bridging. The protection was interesting, too. The cracks in the shale forced unusual nut placements. It was like chess; you had to think. Almost as enjoyable as bouldering. Earlier Freddy had a pitch of the most unlikely laybacking up massive frozen-in (we hoped) jugs.

"It's actually quite rare to get that sort of climbing on big mountains," he enthused, even from fifty metres we could see his grin, "and look, my first nuts in opposition belay!"

"Sounds painful," said the American. "Better not fall off on them."

The summit looked close, though how close, we could not tell. There was no scale to judge by. A narrow ridge ran up to a small ice wall then a whaleback to the apparent top. Large cornices on the right, endless ice slopes to the left. The valleys had long since filled with the daily mist, the wind blew wreaths from left to right, making a Brocken Sceptre of Freddy over the vast and empty space over the East Face. Dick and the Lutheran joined him, disappearing intermittently in the mist.

The sky flickered over Panch Chuli II. Sheets of lightning etched the outline of Nagalaphu on the eyeball. The thunder exploded like surf all round us. I followed the rope up to the others, wondering about it all. I had already felt that familiar and dreadful itching at the ears, the buzz of static, and knew the elemental forces were building up for something unusual. I had almost reached the others when the unusual happened.

The sky ignited overhead: a momentary, almost subliminal whitening of the sky. I felt a sharp pain in my shoulder and side. Someone was trying to electrocute me with a cattle prod. I heard the scream as the electrons tore the air apart over our heads. And I still had those antennae sticking out. I tried to bury the sack in the ice before me, but not before another banshee shrieked across the sky, bringing on more fear and pain and cattle prodding. The other three had been quite unaffected, but then they weren't carrying lightning conductors. The wind had risen, and we were now engulfed in a full storm.

There was no possibility of a bivouac on the ice, but the summit, we thought, might be even more exciting. I feel that at this point in the story I should explain something about lee slopes, cornices and windslab formations, but I shan't. It's too complicated. I'll just say that in the Himalaya cornices are often east-facing, and the snow is usually soft, unstable, and may form interestingly baroque shapes. Somewhere behind us the cornice overhung several large blobs, one of which looked like a tent-sized ledge. Being on the lee side of the slope it would be out of the wind. The problem was one of access, how to bypass the cornice. The team moved down the ridge.

The storm ripped the words from our mouths, we had to communicate in gestures. Freddy, belayed to an ice screw, held the rope while I looked for a safe way down to the enticing ledge. There was a very clear line marking the danger zone, a plating of hard ice on the windward side and softer snow over the cornice. I chose a slight dip in the ridge, perhaps the cornice would be smaller here, and crossed the line. There was a small crevasse on the line. I stepped in the soft snow, nothing happened. I took another step, and leant over to see past the edge. There was a loud report, a thundrous clap, the world collapsed around me, and suddenly I found myself slowly spinning at the end of the rope looking down 600 metres of fluted snow slopes down the East Face. A crescent showed the break in the cornice above, and half our prospective ledge had been carried away too. Life really is a bitch, as they say in BBC English.

We eventually excavated a platform on the windward side of the cornice. The storm blew itself out, as usual, by late evening.

The next day Freddy had formed the opinion that the easiest way to make progress was to follow the fracture line of the cornices. It was hard and icy below the line, while on the cornice itself the snow was soft and level.

I watched Freddy's progress with Dick, who said, "I don't think he should go so close to the edge," and held Freddy's rope tighter. Venables was fifteen metres above us when he appeared to settle, very slowly, in a cloud of snow dust. Dick turned to me as the helmet finally vanished: "He's fallen through the cornice," he said incredulously.

"Oh, is that what's happened? I thought he'd stopped for a cup of tea." Dick would like to have taken a swipe at me but his hands were full, holding the Venables rope tight. Freddy reappeared at the edge, mouthing impeccable BBC. Two hours later we were assembled on the broad summit of Rajrambha.

There was nothing to say. It was just 7.00 a.m. The eastern horizon took us across the border to Nepal, where Api and Kanjiroba glistened under the low sun. Turning west we gazed entranced, as the morning light picked out Nanda Devi, Changabang and Dunagiri: the mountain where it all began. Dick and Joe Tasker. Hard alpine-style climbing. Eleven days. Fifteen years earlier. It made me feel rather humble. Freddy was still taking photographs when the American started down. I waited to follow in Dick's footsteps. And twelve hours later we reached our ABC, 33 metres above Mont Blanc, in the drifting afternoon mists.

We'd been away six days. Chris and Graham had been down to Base and back, and had now gone up Panch Chuli II with Harish's team. Two days later, on 7 June, Muslim Contractor, Monesh Devjani and Pasang Bodh reached their summit, having made the second ascent of the South-West Ridge of Panch Chuli II. The next day Chris and Graham completed their new route on the West Ridge of Panch Chuli II. Both teams had kicked off from a camp at *c.* 6000 metres and had two bivouacs above the bergschrund.

There had been an accident while we were on Rajrambha. Vijay, our Jain, broke his ankle during a huge fall, his crampons must have balled up. He rolled and somersaulted about 300 metres down the Indian Couloir, coming to rest on a slight knoll, a sort of ski jump just above a very deep crevasse. Vijay pointed at the heavens. Shiva, Krishna or perhaps Ganesh had intervened. Then again it may also have had something to do with one of Harish's Manali men, Sundersingh, who fielded Vijay at the last moment, grabbing him before he continued his slide into the bergschrund 100 metres below. Winko had trekked out to Munsiary for the helicopter.

At base the four of us waited for the others to return. In the evening we sprawled out under the red-breasted tent, the divine female floating over us. We talked pub talk, boys' talk. Of Al and Brian in their drinking competitions, the Rab Carrington Patagonian sheep-rustling stories, and how he had now grown up to make down gear and leave expeditions well alone.

Freddy pored over his flower books and identified leaves of the edible Megacarpaea polyandra and the Fritillaria roylei, which grew among the wild garlic at 3400 metres along with the Lilium oxypetalum. "Oxy means sharp. So this must be the sharp-petalled lily." And it was beautifully sharp. Sustad may have become more scarecrow-like throughout the trip, but Dick was looking ever more Neanderthal, like the Quentin Blake drawing from Roald Dahl's *The Twits*. The Lutheran told us of Spewy Hewy, and then another story in the same vein of the Nottingham climber who was seen in the red telephone box, "making a call", with his girlfriend of the evening. The pub windows were plastered with faces looking out at the naked couple. This reminded Freddy and me, at the same moment, of Pasolini's film of the Boccaccio's *Decameron*, where the wife has persuaded her husband to climb into the wine barrel, over the edge of which she leans while the apprentice, her young lover, lifts her skirts. "Scrub harder," exhorts the wife, "and here and here again!" Then we remembered the scene from *Padre Padrone* where the future professor discovers copulation, the farm animals are doing it everywhere he looks, the donkeys, the goats, even the dogs and cats. The peasant boy tries it himself, with a chicken, the camera is obscured by a cloud of feathers flying. "Only trying to collect down!" says Sustad. It took several minutes for calm to return to the pendulous kitchen tent, which swayed in the breeze, the poles creaking like a mast under canvas, which of course is exactly what it was. I stretched out my sleeping bag and dreamt of ships.

Two charred trunks were glowing red under a pan of arra chai, a thick mixture of sugar, milk, tea and *arra* (ginger). An army of rank-and-file cumulus covered the ceiling from the serrated Rajrambha Ridge to the equally serrated Panch Chuli Ridge. Like a vast open-air Greek theatre, the sky was supported on the tips of the pinnacles of the Balati valley. So high were the walls of the theatre that the sun only now reached me, at 8.00 a.m., and I had been up since 5.30, when the dawn touched the peaks. In the background the snout of the glacier resembled a smooth black monolith with two white streams down its face, which contributed to the torrent gushing from a ice cave. White colour, white noise. The birch scrub had grown noticeably leafier around the camp since our arrival.

Harsinh, thin, wiry, small and mongoloid, like my Siberian ancestors, pottered about, head on one side like a bird. I half expected him to peck at the teapot. Instead he picked out a glowing cinder to light his bitter-tasting beedie. Revatram, our cook, brown, tall, thin, hook-nosed, talked with Harsinh in Hindi, their closest common language. Harsinh is from Kumaon, the other from Manali. Revatram asked me if I had seen ibex higher up the mountain, so I tried to describe in sign language the cat tracks we had seen crossing the glacier. Revatram hummed and sighed, "Asah, asah," as he moved the log and settled a clean pan on the flames for kedgeree for lunch. A helicopter flew up the valley towards the intermediate camp, and when it returned fifteen minutes later we guessed that Vijay and Winko were on board. The machine wobbled and floated down to Munsiary.

"Oh damn," said Freddy, "missed the post!"

"That," I observed, "is an interesting association of ideas. A broken ankle, a helicopter, *aha!* a chance to post a letter. It would never have occurred to me."

"It would have eventually," Freddy said.

It was already looking like a successful expedition when the others returned safely for lunch. But we decided to push our luck. We'd have a look at the unclimbed group of Panch Chulis. Maybe this was our mistake.

Chapter Nineteen

Dancing Through the Deodars

From Madkot, the roadhead to the range, there is a spectacular panorama of the Panch Chuli Wall. The view is from the south-west, and in the evening the peaks catch the Alpenglow, ranged in numerical order from II to V. Though II is the highest at 6904 metres, the other peaks attract the mountaineer's ambition. These are steep mixed faces, falling some 2000 metres to the south-flowing Panch Chuli Glacier. This glacier had not been visited by mankind, though the valley, the Pyunshani Gadhera, had seen the occasional hunter from Madkot. From this select group we hired a guide who said he knew the valley, though he didn't tell us till much later that his last visit was more than nine years earlier. The man's name was Dancing.

Dancing had one property that was extremely disconcerting for those of us following. The Lutheran summed it up neatly: "If there's a lone bush in the middle of an open field, he'll walk through it." It was commonplace over the three days it took us to trek to Pyunshani to find Dancing clambering into dense bamboo bushes, while everyone else walked round to meet him on the other side. But we were not to discover this for two days. First the party trekked down to Balati again, where under the deodars we waited for Freddy; he'd last been seen crouching, camera in hand, in the bushes. Soon there was a roaring blundering noise in the jungle undergrowth, like a rhinoceros. But these roaring sounds were Venables: "The bastards, they should have waited, oh, bloody hell, where's the path gone to now? The . . . oh, *hello* everybody. Ah, Victor, did you see the lilac trees? Wonderful aren't they." And I had to admit they were.

We were back in the deodars again, and we wanted to camp there, but Harish said that the next campsite, across the river, was to be just as beautiful.

"How do you know?" I asked.

"Local knowledge, old boy. We have guides, we speak the local language, we are sons of the soils!"

"The soils, old boy?" Sustad grinned from scrawny ear to scrawny ear. Monesh wagged his head till it was fit to fall off. But Harish was right. Across the river was called Phunga Ger, meaning the Flower Pasture. Our tents were set up on a field of strawberries, and orchids and a tall multiflowered thing whose name Freddy told me and which I immediately forgot. I threw my sack down on a euphorbia and squashed it flat. In the background Harish and Monesh were already poring over the maps. Soon the smoke began to trickle skywards from the kitchen. Monesh, neat in his red tracksuit pants, brought apricot Tango in two plastic mugs from the kitchen tent where Revatram checked his watch to see when he should start on the vegetable stew with dumplings.

Inside our tent Muslim and I shared his last beedie. For his honeymoon he had been to the Malayan peninsula and visited not only Kuantan but also Pekan. It was thirty-five years since I had lived there and now the road to Kuantan was a forty-minute drive. It used to be a track and a day's journey. I remembered the convent in Kuantan where we'd been sent to prepare for and receive our first communion. I saw the nuns who fed us soup made from the pastry sheets after the wafers had been pressed out. And I recalled these same nuns believed that rats were male mice. As for Pekan, it was like finding that someone had discovered your private dream, that they too knew the landscape, the palms and the turtle beaches.

Muslim bummed a fresh pair of beedies from Lee Van Cleef, and under a pile of old socks at the bottom of his sack found a half-bottle of Indian whisky.

"What happened to Bhupesh?" I asked.

"He's gone home with Graham." Graham had run out of leave and needed to return to his maps.

"Not too disappointed?"

"No." Mus dragged out the oh till it sounded like a siren. "Nooouuu, it was all very democratic. He volunteered. With a little pushing."

I wondered how Harish had arranged it. Bhupesh was Muslim's

long-standing partner. I'd expected him to top out with Mus on Panch II.

"Tell me the story of your climb. We saw you as small dots while you were ferrying loads up to your Camp 1."

"On the 2nd," Muslim began, "I moved up, Pasang and I stayed up. That's when you saw us. And on the 5th we moved to the col. Everyone came up there, and just Monesh, Pasang and I stayed up there. The col was very windy and the snow was very soft there. (Muslim sighed, breathing heavily as if recalling the altitude.) Six one twenty metres. Above the col we had this rock step going up about 100 metres. Pasang and Monesh fixed this with rope the same day. The next day we were to go up but Pasang had a bad headache. That day was very frustrating for us, we got up at 11.00, were ready to go by 2.00 a.m. But Pasang's headache just wouldn't subside. At this stage we had already decided who was going up."

"When did you decide?" I was enjoying the whisky, and didn't want the story to end too soon.

"The previous day, actually, on the 4th. The weather permitting there was to be a second try, too, Harish and Bhupesh."

"Would Pasang have been with them?"

"Noooe, it would have Harish and Bhupesh alone, or Yograj with them depending on what we told them. Actually it was the first time I climbed with Monesh." Mus took a long toke on the beedie, blowing a fat ring of acrid smoke. With a sip of the whisky he continued.

"At times we were wading through so much deep snow, and suddenly it became icy. All round our camp it was deep snow. After the col we camped on the morning of the 6th at around 6400 metres, where the ridge flattened. We pitched a tent there and stopped for the day. Around 10.30 or something. We took nothing up. No books or anything. There was this uncertainty with Pasang's headache. I was brewing all day. The gas burners were really useful. I couldn't imagine slogging over a kerosene stove. And I was playing nursemaid all day to Pasang with Paracetamol."

"Did you use ice screws?"

"No, except near the top. Just one. Pasang put one in and it bounced out and went down the West Face. It was a tubular one, about the size of the ones you have, they are very broader. That morning we left around five. This is on the 7th. From the Indo-Tibetan Border Police description there was meant to be a large crevasse, but there was a very safe snow bridge across. Then there was some easy angled ice. This must have continued for 100

metres or so to the beginning of the second rock. It wasn't completely
rock, it was mixed, and this took us nearly an hour for three of us
to get over. From the ITBP records, from here there was supposed
to be a big snow plod. But all the snow had gone. It was ice, not
too steep, but very exposed, and this is the time it started getting
cloudy. Before the clouds we could see Chris and Graham on the
West Ridge, so close we could call. We later learned that they
camped near this place at 6700 metres. They had decided to go up
the next morning, you know, to get a good view and photographs.

"Pasang was in the lead on our ridge. We were worried about this
going continuously on ice. Monesh and I had never done anything
like this and took hardly any snaps. We were mentally prepared
to find some snow on top, but we didn't find any. And there was
a terrible wind and these clouds gathering, just below the summit
cornice. That's where Pasang tried to hammer in the ice peg and it
bounced off. The second one went in two inches.

We moved up the last bit. We stopped when we thought we were
near the edge of the cornice and Monesh unroped. He thought he
would go a bit further and stepped through the cornice. His foot just
went through but he pulled it out very quickly. There was no point in
hanging around because there were no views at all. I forgot to tell you
I slipped once just below the summit cornice actually, and I was held
by Pasang. We heard Chris shouting 'Did you do it?' That's when we
realised there was nothing more to do and he yelled congratulations.

And then there was this sense of urgency in getting down. Is that
normal? And now on the higher rock step Monesh and Pasang
hammered in two rock pegs, they just wouldn't let me do anything
on that part. We abseiled down the rocky step. After the abseil we
were completely engulfed in clouds. We took nearly as much time
down as up. Five hours up and four down."

"So what's it like being a tiger at last?"

"Meooow," said Mus, and took another swig of whisky.

Above Phunga Ger was a vertical forest, and next morning Dancing
was forced to use his kukri to cut a path through the bamboo and
rhodedendron, and we had to kick steps in the mud. Freddy slipped
on one of these and a clod of moss flipped up into his eye. "You bastard! These stupid boots have got no tread left, and you all broke the
steps, why didn't you wait?" At which point he noticed that Dancing
was dragging deeply on a beedie. "I say, you haven't got a spare
beedie have you? I'll pay you back from the expedition supply."

"Why, you shameless, helpless . . ." Chris's invective was lost on Freddy who was muttering, "It takes twenty seconds for the nicotine to hit the brain." Sustad had told him that.

Here we found again the macrophylla, the orgasm plant as we called it because each time Freddy saw one he went into a pseudo-sexual paroxysm. "*Aha!* My beautiful macrophylla, have you *ever* seen such a purple . . ." and later he was found crouching over a cluster of flowers ". . . two in front, two behind and one overlapped . . . doesn't mention that in the book . . . Oh, there you are, I'm just counting the leaves on this, they can either be overlapped, in front or behind. This primula has five leaves, I wonder how many variations there are of leaf arrangement."

"With five leaves," I jotted a note in my book, "there can be just three forms. You've got the 2,2,1 form there." But he wasn't listening, he'd found something else:

"This denticulata, look at it, the tiniest primula you'll ever see." I couldn't; he appeared to be staring at a patch of dirt. "Oh, and here's a Megacarpaea . . . It's edible . . ." I tried but it tasted like bitter dandelion and red hot pepper and I had to spit it out. "But first you have to boil it and throw away the water." Oh, thanks, now that I've poisoned myself, he tells me. There was the wild garlic we'd eaten earlier, the tasteless species of strawberries, Daltonia, and other primulas of course.

The Bagarthora Pass was above the tree-line, wide peat bogs sitting above the jungle. And here there were anemones, blue petals with white veins and white petal with a blue tinge. But Freddy was bounding forward again. "Oh and here is our first really red flower, Potentilla atrosanguinea. There's also a white one, looks just like a strawberry with no fruit."

"Pretty useless then, isn't it?" said the American.

I had a sudden and convincing vision of the hairy American on a guided tour of India. And here's the Taj Mahal, what do you think of it? Got no office space? Pretty useless, eh?

Our camp that night, Shyama Gwar, Dockleaf Pasture, was distinguished by a magnificent collection of tiger lilies, though Harish called them cobra lilies, and in truth they did look more like cobras with long whip-like tongues and arched heads about to strike. Revatram was running out of ingredients, and for the third day in a row we ate vegetable stew with dumplings, and in our tent afterwards Muslim began to talk of food. "You know, what I really want, I want a plate of fried eggs. God I'm starved of eggs. Now, shikanji sharbat is very delicious. It is great thing in summer. Sugar, mint, and just a bit of ginger, very little, just a taste, then you boil it, just dissolve the sugar, you heat the water, you add the small piece of ginger at the same time."

Some hunters had been stalking the Panch Chuli valley for five days, and were now returning empty-handed. Two looked like Mongols and had yellow skin, the other was a dark Indo-European with fine ebony features. The 12-bores looked home made. The men were dressed in rags, as seemed to be the local custom, and on their feet were worn-out gym shoes. They looked as if they belonged to the forest. Dancing did not seem to know them, but asked if they knew the way.

Harish reckoned his Manali men were confusing him. We had stopped for lunch, we had already stopped several times while Dancing tried to remember where he was going, and now it was time to get going. "Come on," said Sustad, "time to look for bamboo clumps again."

In the monsoon mists we could sense the presence of large cliffs both above and below us. A gap in the clouds showed a network of steep meadows that seemed to lead to the Panch Chuli valley. Dick set off down this without further reference to the main party. Harish shouted down to us that Dancing said we were going the wrong way. Freddy, Dick and I turned back like recalcitrant sheep. The party was running low on blood sugar. "Why don't you sack him," said Freddy. "He's useless, he's a wanker!" Five minutes later Dancing and the Manali men had stopped again, and this time it was the American who lost his cool. "Don't stop again! What are you, a bunch of little girls?"

On the third day Dancing's route took us down a final section of vertical jungle. With the rucksacks catching on every creeper and vine, we slid down wet cliffs, dangling from bamboo and climbing down a greasy scaffold of rhododendron. Then suddenly we emerged into the open, and blinked in the light. Looking back we could see the canopy ripple as the rest of the team made their way down the vegetated cliff. There was a particularly rapid green wave, a howl, and a great deal of shouting in Hindi, BBC Hindi. Monesh had fallen out of the forest and landed on Harish. A little later the entire team was watching with interest as a lone ripple indicated the peregrinations of Dancing as he looked for an alternative and bushier way out of the jungle.

Chapter Twenty

Panch Chuli V

Chris, Dick, the Stephens and I were surveying Panch Chuli V from a bivouac at 4200 metres. We were tired, having brought up heavy loads 1000 metres from the new Base. We were going to be short of time. We'd have to be back inside five days from Base. We needed a straightforward route, simple route finding, and moderate technical difficulties, preferably with little traversing on brittle ice. And we could see our route. It was to be Panch Chuli V from the South Col. There was an easy summit ridge, and below it a rock buttress that could obviously be turned; we couldn't quite see how, but that didn't worry us. Below the rock was an easy and pleasant-looking cwm. High above the entrance to the cwm there was a lone sérac. The Tower. We did not suppose it posed any great danger. The only niggling doubt was that below the cwm all was hidden from view. We could only guess at what the dead ground might contain, but again chose not to fret about it.

Twenty-four hours later we knew we should have fretted. The two Stephens broke trail across the Maze Glacier while Chris, Dick and I followed them across the icefall we had not been able to see. It was ugly, tortured ground. First their tracks led across The Splits, an unstable arch of iceblocks, which needed wide bridging to avoid overloading the central span, averting eyes from the chasm below. Next the footprints wandered very slowly under the Venus Fly Trap, a weird overhang fringed with ice fangs. Then there was the Long Jump, slightly downhill, we'd not be able to reverse that. The enchanted Maze followed. In bad weather this section could be impossible without millions of marker wands. Later there was the Double Snowbridge, a traverse over that most unstable of structures, two bridges holding each other up, then a final section under innocuous-looking ice ramparts, whose detritus belied their looks. The whole thing added up to four hours wandering about in a minefield. Dick, Chris and I followed the tracks feeling both horrified and impressed.

"Really interesting ground," said Freddy when we reached their bivi site.

"Really frightening," said I. "So here we are in the Mouth of the Cauldron. Must be about five two, no?"

Above us the Tower began to look a little threatening. Fresh avalanche tracks swept down from the slopes under it and through the Cauldron over the ice cliffs below. Freddy and the Lutheran had chosen a site by a wide-mouthed crevasse where the avalanche tracks bifurcated. The whole of the Cauldron was tilted at 30 degrees, perfect slab-avalanche country. I was beginning to get bad feelings about the valley. We all were. And outside the tents was the most beautiful ever-changing cloudscape, a thick black ceiling, the sun creeping under to illuminate white cumulus towers and, at dusk, a huge anvil over Munsiary with sheet lightning underneath.

We set the alarms for four, but long before that our tent was buffeted, and I thought that Freddy was throwing snowballs at us. Dick was far too grown up to do that. But it wasn't Freddy, it was the sérac. Blocks had broken away from the tower. Fortunately, we were not in the main fall-line, but should a major collapse occur in the Tower, there was little doubt in our minds that our bivouac would be obliterated. This thought lent some urgency to our preparations. Chris, the American and I scraped the ice condensate from the side of the tent as we hurriedly dressed, slurped at the pan of boiling tea, burning our chapped lips, and pulled icy boots onto our cold feet. We shook out the crusty tents, our mittened hands clumsy in their grip.

There was a prolonged argument about whether we should run away while we packed our sacks. Freddy wanted to go on, someone had suggested a rest day the night before, but that did not seem so attractive now. We came to a compromise, we'd climb to the col at the head of the Cauldron. This would place us at about 5800 metres, within striking distance of the top for a day's outing. This was a group decision.

Dick broke trail, deep brittle crust, till we had passed from under the Tower, which I noted had thirteen bands of dark and thirteen bands of light ice. It was, I supposed, thirteen years old.

Just when we thought we were safe, a large single block of ice bounced and crashed down the face above us, passing between Sustad and Chris.

Chris said, "Christ, you know this is bloody nonsense. I really think we should think about what we're doing."

But Venables was in no mood for discussion.

"What, are you creating again?"

"Sometimes, I think you are a very selfish man."

"Take no notice, Chris," I said. "He doesn't mean it. He'll be fine in ten minutes." Then I added, "But if you want I'll go down with you."

"Thank you, that gives me the support I need to go on."

Perverse bugger, I thought, just when I could see a way to escape this nightmare. The snow crust was still horribly slow, and yet we had the Sword of Damocles hanging above us. Argh.

We were on the South Col at about 5850 metres, leaving us with just 600 metres for the day trip to the summit. We reckoned we'd be back the next morning by 9 a.m. It was true that we'd be out of food the next day, but that didn't matter, we'd be on the way down. It was more worrying that the Tower had begun to lose material. We were finishing our lunch, a soup brew and a packet of instant mash, when a *vroooooom* attracted our attention. A spectacular climax avalanche was sweeping our tracks out of the Cauldron. Another followed it five minutes later. *Vroooooom*. It sound just like Concorde taking off. The avalanche swept into the mouth of the Cauldron and up the other side.

"There goes last night's bivi," said Freddy, wiping a minute blob of instant mash from his beard and back into his mouth. I wondered who bought the stuff in England. It's vile, I just could not imagine giving up real potatoes for this. Perhaps people buy it for wallpaper paste. Not only were we almost out of food, there was also a shortage of smokes. The American found some tobacco which he dredged from his pockets, ten per cent tobacco, ninety per cent fluff. There were no papers, so he carefully rolled up a tomato soup packet and poured the fluffy dust into the end.

"I learnt this from Doug, while he was going through one of his non-smoking times . . . Hey, Venables!" he called to the other tent. "If you're desperate for nicotine, this works!" He puffed away at the soup packet, making a foul stench, then shouted out to the other tent again.

"Dick! If we get up this mountain, can I have one of your Gitanes?"

"Hmmm, only got one left."

"What about a couple of drags then?"

I sat huddled in my bag trying to rise above the eccentric behaviour of my companions, sipping delicious rosehip tea, flavoured with Complan, vile mash and garlic soup. It snowed gently, as it did every afternoon. The morning weather had been incredible, with dark, dust-laden air over Munsiary and all land to the south. And here on the col, on the watershed, the Panch Chuli chain, having basked in clear sun all morning, slowly sank under the tide washing up from the foothills. A wall of cloud was rolling in, fluffy white pillows floating on the solid mass of dark air.

Sustad was looking forward to the next day. Two or three hundred metres of steep mixed climbing should take us onto a gentle summit ridge. Given reasonable weather, it should be enjoyable. A short day. He was very wrong.

When the alarm went off at 2.00 a.m. Chris announced his decision to stay put and wait for us. He was unusually tired, and felt he'd only hold us up. Perhaps it was also a case of the survival instinct which has served Chris so well over the years coming into play. Always listen to your instinct. It's what keeps mountaineers alive. Back at Base, Muslim watched Harsinh making a pan of tea, which fell from the fire, dousing the flames. Harsinh looked up horrified. "Bad sign," he said, backing off. "They are in great danger."

"It's going to be a long day," said Dick. The steep mixed ground between the pillars had already taken us much longer than we'd allowed. It was now 10.30 a.m.

The Lutheran had put in one blindingly good lead, the crux of which was an open corner. We watched him sweeping the snow from the smooth rock with his arm, looking for minuscule footholds and tiny cracks in the granite for his axes. It was serious, his nearest runner was a poor nut fifteen metres below. It took an hour for him to edge and balance his way up the ten-metre section. But even the easier ground had taken time. We had had to place runners in almost every pitch. Now we were at the top of the steep buttress, where we had expected to be walking.

"That's not snow, it's ice. We'll be traversing that on front points." Dick continued. "That's the South Summit there, we can't see the main top. And we'll need to be at the top by twelve if we're to get down in daylight."

It would be almost half a kilometre to the south top. The clouds rolled in and enveloped and separated us like lost souls. Slowly we crept along the ice, staying well clear of the cornice. Kick and balance, no mistakes, please. Hammer, stab, kick, kick. Rest. Hammer, stab. Slow, slow, tired.

Here was the South Summit, swirling mists.

"I'm worried," I said to Freddy, meaning I was tired and worried. "It's two o'clock, and we've got four hours traversing on front points to reverse from here. If we go down now we'll probably not get down before midnight."

"Come on, Victor, look, there's the summit." A pale pyramid materialised in the swirls then disappeared again. "I haven't come all this way to turn back now."

"Look, we've taken far too long already," I said.

"All right," said Dick, "why don't we go on for just an hour."

"Right," said Freddy. "It's two now. We go on till three, then we'll definitely turn back."

"Definitely?"

"Yes, definitely."

"OK."

We reached the top at 3.09 p.m. on 20 June.

Dick said: "The odds were stacked against us getting to this summit."

"Still are stacked against us." I must have sounded depressed. I wasn't, merely anxious to get down. The afternoon clouds shrouded us and the mountain. We knew Chris would have expected us back by now. It was not till midnight that he saw our headtorches. He had been desperately worried, and now he was able to relax. He put on a giant brew.

Freddy and I watched the others go down. We had had no food or water for the last twenty-three hours. It was 2.00 a.m., eleven hours since we set foot on the summit, but after this abseil there would only be one more to the tent and that brew we felt sure Chris would be making.

Freddy said: "I am really pleased we pulled this one off, Victor."

"We're not down yet." Not intended as any kind of put-down, more a form of neurosis on my part. Abseils have always terrified me. Gingerly I stepped off the ledge and loaded the ropes. The anchor was a good-looking short angle, driven to the hilt in a horizontal crack. There were two back-up nuts. Nothing to worry about there. I turned the torch down into the void and began to dangle.

Freddy had seen two of us safely down, and began to remove the back-up while I was still on the rope. It was obviously safe. Dick and Sustad were not too sure about the next anchor, and were still adding to it when I arrived. Dick threaded a rope end through the abseil sling. Sustad was groping about in the dark for yet another nut placement. It was 2.30 a.m. Chris turned the gas off, he'd reheat the brew when we got down.

Freddy stepped off his ledge and began down. He'd been a little violent in loading the rope, but it was OK, for about five metres. Then he entered the "dream sequence". "Look!" Dick, Sustad and I turned towards the crashing sound. A large squarish black shadow skidded past trailing a shower of sparks. It looked like stonefall.

"His anchor's gone!" In that instant we all knew it was true. That was no stonefall, those sparks were made by crampons. Silence for a moment, for an eternity. The ropes! I grabbed the tangle of ropes before me just as they began to whip through in pursuit of Venables. They shredded trousers and my gloves, but it was Dick who stopped them leaving the belay. Dick held the seventy-metre fall in his gloved hands, with just one turn of the rope through our anchor.

Chris heard the noise, and watched the falling headtorch, as it bounced down to the glacier. One of them's gone, he thought. Tears filled his eyes.

Venables thought he had gone too. "I hadn't connected the dream sequence with the abseil. It was only afterwards I thought Ah, yes, the anchor's come out. I think that was on the way down. So many thoughts . . . as I somersaulted and cartwheeled. I felt, Ah God, how can my body put up with this violence, so loud and crashing." He fell through a vertical twenty-five-metre section, across a slab, and down another twenty-five-metre wall.

"I am holding his whole weight, can't do it much longer," gasped Dick. I fumbled for my prusik loops and put a klemheist on both ropes which Sustad connected to the anchor. The ends could now be freed to tie into the belay. We were shouting to Venables all the while, no answer. I'd begun to think the worst when a distant shout could be heard. "Is anyone there?" He too had been shouting. I wondered if we had been synchronised, and waiting for replies during the same interval.

Sustad had added to the belay, and we felt confident that it would take the weight of two at least. I prusiked down the tight rope till I could see the huddled shadow at the end of the rope.

"I think I've broken my legs." Dick heard that, and wondered if that really meant he couldn't feel his legs, and had in fact broken his back. Venables had hit the knot at the end of the rope at the same time as he had reached the icefield above the bergschrund. His head and back were, miraculously, untouched. There was a lot of blood, spreading like a halo into the snow around him. A sort of red chromatograph.

"If I don't make it, will you say sorry to Rosie and . . ."

"Don't be ridiculous, of course you're going to make it."

A quick examination produced a great deal of howling and a suggestion that he had a broken left ankle, an open fracture near the right knee, and chest injuries. He looked a mess. It was not at all clear to me that he was going to survive the next few hours. But the main thing was to get him off the mountain, that and stop the bleeding.

I fixed up a belay and dug out a large ledge for the broken legs, to get them high, reduce the pressure and bleeding. The others started down, showering us with ice chips and gravel. The chief problem was the right leg, which I splinted with the Karrimat from our Macsacs, then inserted the splinted leg into the rucksack which was attached to the rope above Venables' head with a jumar. It would allow him to control the amount of support to the limb. This was important as my trusty Gregson Pack only had Paracetamol, and I decided the best way to control the pain was not to introduce unnecessary movement to the legs. I have to say, distasteful as it is to commend one's friends, that for a hypochondriac, Venables was incredibly brave. The pain of the next twelve hours was clearly excruciating. Dick and I took turns to lower him down the 400-metre slope to the bergschrund. Sustad soloed off to tell Chris the news and the two of them packed up the tents and started climbing down. About 150 metres above the schrund Bonington chose to cartwheel. His crampons must have balled up, he slid, tried to brake, caught his front points in the ice and lost it completely. He cartwheeled down in twenty-metre bounds. Head, heels, head, heels, axes flailing. He shot over the schrund trying to curl up into a ball, with the idea that he'd be less likely to break his limbs if they weren't sticking out. Ingenious.

Dick saw it all. Chris coming to rest, sitting up, and holding his head in his hands for ages. When Dick joined me he was looking pale and was climbing very very carefully. Sustad reached the Cauldron and helped Chris cut out a platform and erected the tents. Chris tried again with the waiting brew scenario. This time it worked, though we were not to reach the tents till 3 p.m. – almost thirty-six hours after we had left our bivi on the South Col.

The next morning Chris and Sustad went down to summon help, leaving us three and a half cylinders of gas, three packets of the dreaded instant mash and a few packets of soup. They reached base the same afternoon. Chris went on the next day and, using kukris to cut their way out of the jungle, walked out with Harsinh Senior (who now knew his tea pan had not lied) in a blistering nine hours. It would normally have been a three-day effort.

The tent we shared with Freddy had a pool of blood under the Karimats. It smelled as an abattoir smells. You read about the smell of blood, you associate it with hospitals and war, but you'll never be prepared for it. All body fluids smell strongly. After a day or two blood becomes as rank and sharp as sweat, or urine. I helped Dick reshape the snow ledge under Freddy, to support the legs. We aired his sleeping bag which dried quickly in the morning sun. The dried blood was far less noxious, though it did make the bag rather stiff and crinkly. Although we had little food, Venables still had the problem of shitting. We could barely move him into and out of his sleeping bag, let alone a good distance from the tent. We tried to persuade him not to do it any more, but he was not going to be constipated by reason. The solution we arrived at was the Wilkinson Method, a particularly nauseating practice of Dave Wilkinson who is wont to employ the cooking pot and put it outside to freeze solid overnight, when the contents can be tapped free in the morning. It works. But I'll draw a veil over that particular scene. Life on mountains may be beautiful, but it can also be disgusting when mankind gets there.

It was going to be a long wait. Would a helicopter make it here? We hoped so. The idea of manhandling Freddy down the Maze Glacier was worrying. We couldn't possibly do it without a large team, and Dick and I couldn't leave him for more than a few hours. He needed us to help in almost everything.

Dick told us of his dream during the walk-in.

"It was one of those really vivid dreams. We were climbing with people whom I knew but didn't know. One of them looked like Mark, but he wasn't Mark. There was this other climber, he was soloing quite a hard route. I think we were soloing, but a much easier one. Very steep limestone. He fell without any warning. I remember that horrible sound of flesh hitting rock. We watched the fall; it was steep rock, but he bounced off it before landing on the steep ground below. It was very difficult to reach him, we had to do a pendulum. The man was really smashed up. When I reached him he said, 'I'm going to be all right, aren't I?' 'Yes, you're going to be fine,' I said, then he just died.''

"Ahh . . . Chrrrrrrr . . . Shhhhhhh . . . Ahh . . . Chrrrrrrr . . . Shhhhhhh.'' Venables was snoring on a pillow of duvet jackets. His arms folded across his pigeon chest and his glasses pushed uncomfortably up his enormous forehead. The chestnut beard and moustache emphasised his thin face. I took his glasses off the scarred nose and hung them where he could easily reach them. His Ganesh medal hung out of his shirt, and I pushed it back in. I believe I forgot myself so far as to stroke his poor head. It was snowing outside. Dick and I fretted about the rescue operation. Chris said he would set in motion a land operation involving the ITBP, at the same time as calling for a chopper. But the thing that worried us now was food. If it continued snowing, Dick and I would be trapped in this Cauldron with Freddy. The avalanche danger was just too great to risk going down to collect. We wondered if someone would think to chopper a food drop in, if they couldn't pick Venables up.

"And even if a chopper can fly to this altitude, will there be the weather window?''

While Chris and Harish telephoned for the helicopter at Munsiary, Sustad rested a day, then carried a load of food and gas 1800 metres up to a broad ridge at *c.*5000 metres with Harsinh Junior. This operation took two days. The American was exhausted, and had to solo the last 400-metre gully at night. Dick and I collected the food four days after the accident. We had shared the last dreadful little packet of dehydrated potato with Venables, and left him a quarter-cylinder of gas in case we didn't return. It was no more than a gesture.

On the broad ridge was Sustad's rucksack. There was a note left on the food:

Sorry for the low volume of food. It's all we had at Base Camp (barring some onions) & it's also all I could carry on my own. Should have fresh supplies in 2 days at base and so it will be 4 days from now till next delivery. Bottom icefall is now very dangerous. At ⅔ on way down turn sharp right at flattish area into centre of icefield & then down. Be careful. Heli could come any time. Sorry no books. I am just too weak to carry much more. Hope all is well. You're in my thoughts, Stephen.

Under the note were potatoes, tinned fish, sugar, tea and gas cylinders. But better than all that, the chopper was on its way! We set up a stove and made a huge brew, and ate a tin of fish. Although we only had to climb 600 metres back to the tent, we thought we might not have the strength to do this without the food.

In addition to the climb there was the sheer fright of passing under the Tower. Some instinct had made us go down for the food a few hours earlier than seemed sensible. This meant that we'd be climbing back up to the tent at 3.00 a.m. rather than 7.00 a.m. The whole operation would have to take place in the dark. But some small voice, a sixth sense, instinct, call it what you will, had told us to go, and go soon. It was not logical, but we'd both heard the voice before.

Dick broke trail at heartbursting pace in order to pass through the danger zone under the Tower. We had just crossed this when the whole face of the sérac began to break up. With a roar the avalanche swept across the Cauldron, up the other side of the valley, and on into the glacier beyond. Horrified, I looked at how much of our track was left. About five minutes' worth. The Tower continued to disintegrate for the next four hours. As I followed Dick up the rest of the Cauldron, I fancied I could hear him muttering to himself, something about always listening to your instincts . . .

The helicopter flew in in the afternoon. We were at 5600 metres, which is pretty damn close to the flying ceiling for Alouettes. There was no winch, presumably to save weight, and so the pilots had to attempt a half-landing. They hovered five metres from us and motioned their requirements. It was like trying to communicate with gods in a maelstrom. Dick lay on the collapsed tents to stop them blowing away. I clutched at Freddy to stop him tobogganing down the slope in his sleeping bag. Now that would have been embarrassing. The chopper put one skid down on the outside edge of the tent platform, the rotor tips inches from the snow, and not much more above our heads. One mistake from the pilots, and Freddy and I would be salamied. A door opened, the co-pilot motioned, I pushed and Venables pulled. He landed his torso on the floor behind the pilots. The aircraft wandered slightly, the co-pilot gestured violently. In desperation Venables put his broken ankle on the skid and pushed off on it, I heaved in the general direction of the cockpit. With a howl of pain Venables shot into the cabin, clutching his groin with one hand. The door wouldn't close, but he was mostly inside the bubble. I collapsed exhausted. The chopper wobbled uncertainly and moved off. The leg withdrew, the Perspex door shut. The pilots waved and turned for home.

Dick and I staggered into Base Camp at 10.00 p.m. It had taken us nine hours to descend from the Cauldron. It was dark and we had been lost for over an hour, wandering around over the shrub-covered ravines till Dick recognised a boulder-edged stream. Harsinh Junior and Prakash took our sacks from us. Sustad hugged us like long-lost family: "Thank God! Oh, thank God you're here!" Prakash got down on his hands and knees to blow the fire and make more tea.

Then we slept till the sun fell on our faces and the scent of plants and the music of small birds and animals awoke us. I remembered how we had woken to the mechanical sound of the chopper the day before. Dick and I had dragged Venables out in his sleeping bag, and laid him out in the snow. "It looks just like an insect," he said. A metal dragonfly, I had thought, dangling under diaphanous rotors, the bulbous cockpit like a huge compound eye. The pilot and co-pilot in helmet, oxygen masks and dark glasses had looked inhuman (though I knew they ate dhal and rice). The machine had flown round the Cauldron, to taste the air currents. Helicopters are so frighteningly noisy. Then the smell of parathas and coffee brought us on a day and made us rise.

Chapter Twenty-one

Beer

Dick, Sustad and I, with Harish's three Manali men, walked out of the Panch Chuli valley in two days. There were still deodars and rhododendrons and flowers, but somehow without Freddy to tell us what we were looking at it just wasn't the same, except when, nearing Ringo again, we crossed Lampata Karsu, the Long Clearing, which was like a wildlife park, with troops of wild monkeys swirling through the branches like hooligans, and deer and wild boar. To Madkot, the town of the Blank Stare, then by truck to Munsiary where the others were waiting, and the evil bus to Delhi, where we had news of Freddy. Muslim had seen him off from Delhi Airport, where his last tantrum on Indian soil was thrown.

Freddy had assumed he'd be travelling business class, but once he had been wheeled out onto the tarmac they told him that they weren't sure they'd be able to carry him up the stairs to business class. Not only that, the flight crew had not been consulted, and he could not be loaded without their permission. Harish had a friend in Customs who, behind the scenes, came to the poor man's aid by refusing to clear the flight without Venables aboard. But Freddy knew nothing of this and began to get very, very angry. "This is a disgrace! I'll never fly Air India again!" and so on. Muslim looked on astonished. So did the flight crew.

"Perhaps he should try meditation," someone said afterwards.

Yes, Tantric meditation, I thought.

Bombay Airport, and Sustad was badly in need of a haircut and shave, the usual thing after expeditions. He looked like one of the

Husbands From Hell, a programme beamed by satellite to the utterly bemused audience in Bombay. From the ground up, Sustad wore brothel creepers, black socks, yellow and orange bermuda shorts, and a tee shirt with a white paint-can mark over the belly, before you came to the horrible chin stubble and long uncombed hair. Bonington asked him to stand behind a pillar in case he disturbed the check-in girl. We had twenty pieces of baggage. The girl called her boss over, a thin man with a photolabel on his lapel.

"You have got 290 kilos, which is . . ." He scribbled on a pad. "115 kilos over . . .'

"Well there should be a telex from London . . ." Chris interrupted very convincingly.

"I did not receive one."

"I am sure there should be one, my office contacted London, I am absolutely sure . . ."

"I am not charging you." The man could not bear to see Chris suffer any longer. "I am not charging you, just informing you that you are 115 kilos over." He smiled. We were a source of amusement. We need not have hidden Sustad after all.

"Hey!" We turned around. "Hey!" A seated man and woman were calling to us.

"Hello, Pat," Chris exclaimed.

"Pat and Baiba Morrow!" I had not seen them since they tried to run me over with mountain bikes in Baltit. Before that we met on Elbrus when Pat was completing the Seven Summits tour. "What you doing?"

"We're on our way to Ladakh, to trek from Leh through Zanskar to God knows where. It's some kind of photographic scam. We've flown from Toronto, across the Pacific."

"Just to meet us here?"

In the Jumbo, I looked into the cockpit where the ground engineers were playing with the knobs. Overhead the letters H MALAYA were stencilled.

"What's that?" I asked.

"That is the name of the aircraft, Himalaya." Oh, good, that seems auspicious. The cockpit door opened. A fat red tube was pushed into the tiny technical space. Followed by an arm with captain's rings on the cuff pushing the golf bag. The pilot smiled at me:

"I'm going to London for a spot of go'f."

"And I'm going for a beer," I said.

What looked like the big brother of Scottish deer fencing was no doubt electrified. The fence defined the edge of the runway, and kept the shanty town at bay with its muddy, refuse-strewn alleys, the crowded families and their animals. In a corner used for toilet functions, the children played cricket. Through the porthole the scene slipped away.

Beer in hand, I fell asleep and dreamt. I was back at Balati. Above our Base there was the hill we called the Lump, or the Hill of Flowers. It was covered in flowers. There were brown curled ferns and black ones too. There were metre-high Megacarpaea and huge umbellifers, a confusion of dock leaves and sorrels and grasses and parsley-like umbellifers. Marsh marigolds were scattered around springs and streams like gold sovereigns. Dick saw six doves on the hill. He lay back in the sun. "I'm really kicking myself for not bringing the paints. I thought we'd just dash there and back . . . must get out of this dashing habit." Butterflies danced in couples, while small wasps and flies buzzed, and a dark shadow arced low and flashed past in search of its lunch.

I close the fingers of my outstretched hand round the smooth glass. Amber beer and cream. Pedigree. It is a good local, the oak-panelled Nobody Inn. There's not much choice on Newington Green. We are lucky, and there is always the exceptional Lucknow, should you feel the need to float a decent curry on your beer. There is an old-fashioned red telephone kiosk on the corner. Down the steps a punkette in black leathers points out selections for her friend with the electrified hair, and leans her body across the juke box. I can't help being reminded of Boccaccio.

The swing doors slam open. Enter Sustad, clean shaven. What a shock, he looks like a seventeen-year-old again. The juke box goes country and western.

"And will it be a pint of bitter?" I ask over the music.

"Of course. Any news?"

"Yes, Freddy is in Bath Hospital. His left ankle has been pinned, I think he's got a fracture of the medial maleolus, same as me. The right tibia had a bit knocked off its head, that was the open fracture producing all the blood. The kneecap was shattered. They'll wire it together again once they've dug out the wee bits, and they say that his chest is undamaged, just bruised. What about you?"

"Oh, just fine, back to the workshop in Shropshire tomorrow. I'll be working on Julian's house. Any news of Dick?"

"I imagine Dick will be supporting sculpting with abseil work again. He's due in town next week. And Chris has gone canoeing in France with Wendy. According to the news, the lorry drivers have blocked all major routes through the country. Have you seen the television?"

"No."

"France is one enormous traffic jam. I think their best hope of using the canoe is to put it on the top of the Volvo and sit in it, admiring the French countryside from the peaceful silence of the motionless motorway."

Sustad sees the pen and book.

"You are diarising again, I bet you're writing all kinds of nasty things about me."

"I am, my friend, I am . . ."

Index